90 Days in the Word for BUSINESS PROFESSIONALS

ONE MINUTE BIBLE

90 Days in the Word for BUSINESS PROFESSIONALS

ONE MINUTE BIBLE

Daily Devotions That Bring God's Word to the Business World

HOLMAN
REFERENCE

Nashville, Tennessee

One Minute Bible–*Business Professionals*
Copyright © 1999 Broadman & Holman Publishers
Nashville, Tennessee, 37234
All rights reserved

0-8054-9363-8
Dewey Decimal Classification: 242.68
Subject Heading: BUSINESSPEOPLE PRAYER

Production Staff
Executive Editor: David Shepherd
Editor: Lawrence Kimbrough
General Editor: David Goetz, Leadership Resources, Christianity Today, Inc.
Project Editor: Lloyd Mullens
Design Team: Wendell Overstreet, Anderson Thomas Graphics
Typesetting: TF Designs
Production: Kevin Kunce

Library of Congress Cataloging-in Publication Data
One-minute Bible : ninety days in the Word for business professionals
    p. cm.
  ISBN 0-8054-9363-8
  1. Businesspeople Prayer–books and devotions–English. 2. Devotional calendars. I. Title.
BV4596.B8K53   1999
242'.68–dc21   99-15735
                                                                        CIP

Printed in United States of America
1 2 3 4 5 6 04 03 02 01 00 99
[R]

CONTRIBUTORS

M. Craig Barnes is pastor of National Presbyterian Church in Washington, D.C. He is author of *Yearning* and *When God Interrupts*.

Roger Barrier is senior pastor of Casas Adobes Baptist Church in Tucson, Arizona. He is author of *Listening to the Voice of God*.

Ken Blanchard is a management consultant and has worked with Chevron, Lockheed, AT&T, and other major corporations. He is author of *The One-Minute Manager* and *We Are the Beloved: A Spiritual Journey*.

Richard Nelson Bolles is a vocational counselor and author of *The 1998 What Color Is Your Parachute?*, *How to Find Your Mission in Life*, and *How to Create a Picture of Your Ideal Job or Next Career*.

Jill Briscoe is director of "Telling the Truth" media ministry and editor of *Just Between Us*, a magazine for ministry wives and women in ministry. A popular conference speaker, she is author of more than forty books.

Bob Buford is chairman of the board and CEO of Buford Television, Inc., a Texas-based cable TV company. He is founder of Leadership Network, an organization that connects pastors of large churches. He is author of *Half-Time* and *Game Plan*.

Lynn Buzzard is professor of constitutional law at Campbell University School of Law in North Carolina and has co-authored *Church Hiring & Volunteer Selection* and *Mediation-Arbitration: A Reader*.

Kennon Callahan is a church consultant and author of *Twelve Keys to an Effective Church*, *Effective Church Finances*, *Effective Church Leadership*, and *Dynamic Worship*.

Max De Pree is chairman of the board at Herman Miller, Inc. He has been named by *Fortune* to the National Business Hall of Fame. He is author of *Leadership Is an Art* and *Leadership Jazz*.

James Dobson is president and founder of Focus on the Family. He is author of *Love Must Be Tough*, *Life on the Edge*, *Love for a Lifetime*, and *The New Dare to Discipline*.

Peter Drucker is founder of the Peter F. Drucker Foundation for Nonprofit Management. He teaches management and social science at the Claremont Graduate School in Claremont, California. He is author of *The Effective Executive* and *The New Realities*.

Terry Fullam served as rector of St. Paul's Episcopal Church, Darien, Connecticut, for seventeen years. He has written *Living the Lord's Prayer*, *How to Walk with God*, *Riding the Wind*, and *Fit for God's Presence*.

Mark Galli is editor of *Christian History* magazine. Before that he was associate editor with *Leadership Journal*. He is author of *Preaching That Connects*.

George H. Gallup, Jr., is president of the Gallup Poll and executive director of the Gallup Organization, Inc. in Princeton, New Jersey.

Carl F. George is a church consultant and author of *Prepare Your Church for the Future* and co-author of *The Coming Church Revolution* and *Leading and Managing Your Church*.

David L. Goetz is editor of Leadership Resources for Christianity Today, Inc. He is general editor of the "Pastor's Soul" series and the "Building Church Leaders" notebook, and has written for *Christianity Today* and *Christian History*.

Os Guinness is a theologian and writer. He is author of *The American Hour* and *The Calling*.

Richard Halverson, who died in 1995, was a former U.S. Senate chaplain and longtime pastor of Fourth Presbyterian Church near Washington, D.C.

David Hansen is pastor of Belgrade Community Church in Belgrade, Montana. He is author of *The Art of Pastoring* and *The Power of Loving Your Church*.

Mark O. Hatfield is a longtime senator from Oregon.

Robert Hudnut is pastor of Winnetka Presbyterian Church in suburban Chicago. He is author of *This People, This Parish*.

Bill Hybels is founder and senior pastor of Willow Creek Community Church. He is author of *The God You're Looking For, Fit to Be Tied*, and *Too Busy Not to Pray*.

Glen Kehrein is a pastor of Rock of Our Salvation Free Church in Chicago, Illinois.

Jay Kesler is president of Taylor University and author of *Being Holy, Being Human*.

Bruce Larson was for many years the pastor of University Presbyterian Church in Seattle, Washington. He is author of *No Longer Strangers* and *The Relational Revolution*.

Craig Brian Larson is pastor of Lake Shore Assembly of God in Chicago, Illinois, and editor of *Preaching Today* and PreachingToday.com. He is author of *Pastoral Grit* and *Hanging on Till the Better End*.

Steve Mathewson is senior pastor of Dry Creek Bible Church in Belgrade, Montana. He is a regular contributor to *Leadership Journal* and contributing writer to *Building Church Leaders* and the Quest Study Bible. He has also been a featured preacher on *Preaching Today*.

John Maxwell is founder and president of Injoy, Inc., an institute for developing leaders. Before that, he was pastor at Skyline Wesleyan Church in Lemon Grove, California. He is author of *Developing the Leader Within You, Developing the Leaders Around You*, and *The 21 Irrefutable Laws of Leadership*.

Donald McCullough is president of San Francisco Theological Seminary (PCUSA) and is author of *The Trivialization of God* and *Finding God in the Most Unlikely Places*.

Mark Mittelberg is executive vice president of the Willow Creek Association. He is co-author of *Becoming a Contagious Christian* book and training course.

Mark Moring is editor of *Computing Today*. Before that he was an editor with *Campus Life* magazine.

Danny Morris is director of developing ministries with The Upper Room, a discipleship wing of the United Methodist Church in Nashville, Tennessee. He is author of *Yearning to Know God's Will* and *A Life That Really Matters*.

Elizabeth Cody Newenhuyse is a writer living in the Chicago area. She is a contributing editor to *Today's Christian Woman* and the author of *Sometimes I Feel Like Running Away from Home* and *God, I Know You're Here Somewhere*.

Henri Nouwen, who died in 1996, was a theologian who taught at Yale, Harvard, and Notre Dame. He wrote of *The Wounded Healer, The Return of the Prodigal,* and *Our Greatest Gift*.

Lloyd John Ogilvie is the chaplain for the United States Senate. Before that, he was pastor of First Presbyterian Church of Hollywood.

John Ortberg is a teaching pastor at Willow Creek Community Church. He is author of *The Life You've Always Wanted* and *Love Beyond Reason*.

J. I. Packer is professor emeritus at Regent College in Vancouver, British Columbia, and senior editor of *Christianity Today*. He is author of *Knowing God*.

Ben Patterson is dean of the chapel at Hope College in Holland, Michigan. He is author of *Waiting: Finding Hope When God Seems Silent* and *Deepening Your Conversation with God*.

Ted Roberts is pastor of East Hill Foursquare Church in Gresham, Oregon.

Haddon Robinson holds the Harold J. Ockenga chair of preaching at Gordon-Conwell Theological Seminary in South Hamilton, Massachusetts. He is author of *Biblical Preaching* and co-author of *A Voice in the Wilderness*.

Ed Rowell is editor of *Proclaim, Let's Worship,* and *Growing Churches*. Before that he was an associate editor with *Leadership Journal* and editor of *Preaching Today*. He is author of *Preaching with Spiritual Passion*.

Bob Shank reaches the business and professional community through Priority Living, which he founded in 1984. Before entering vocational ministry, he worked in the construction industry. Bob is author of *Total Life Management*.

Fred Smith, Sr. is a business executive living in Dallas, Texas. He is a recipient of the Lawrence Appley Award of the American Management Association. He is author of *You and Your Network*, *Learning to Lead*, and *Leading with Integrity*.

Joni Eareckson Tada is founder of JAM Ministries, a parachurch organization located in Augoura Hills, California, that advocates the cause of, and ministers to, those with disabilities. She is author of *Heaven* and *More Precious than Silver*.

Dallas Willard is professor of philosophy at University of Southern California. He is author of *The Spirit of the Disciplines* and *The Divine Conspiracy*.

William H. Willimon is dean of the chapel at Duke University. He is author of *Resident Aliens*, *Where Resident Aliens Live*, and *Peculiar Speech*.

Ravi Zacharias is a Christian apologist and author of *Can Man Live Without God?*

Zig Ziglar is a motivational speaker and author of *See You at the Top*, *Over the Top*, and *Confessions of a Grieving Christian*.

TABLE OF CONTENTS

GOD'S GOLDEN PARACHUTE

IN MANY CORPORATE MERGERS, THE TOP EXECUTIVES END UP WITH A GOLDEN PARA-
CHUTE; THE REST OF THE EMPLOYEES PLUMMET TO EARTH. RAW DEALS ARE OFTEN
PART OF BIG DEALS. THE OLD TESTAMENT CHARACTER JOSEPH HAD A STRING OF
RAW DEALS. HIS BROTHERS SOLD HIM LIKE A SLAVE TO EGYPT, YET JOSEPH DIDN'T
RETALIATE WHEN HE CAME INTO POWER.

GENESIS 50:15-21

When Joseph's brothers saw that their father was dead, they said, "What if Joseph holds a grudge against us and pays us back for all the wrongs we did to him?"

So they sent word to Joseph, saying, "Your father left these instructions before he died: 'This is what you are to say to Joseph: I ask you to forgive your brothers the sins and the wrongs they committed in treating you so badly.' Now please forgive the sins of the servants of the God of your father." When their message came to him, Joseph wept.

His brothers then came and threw themselves down before him. "We are your slaves," they said.

But Joseph said to them, "Don't be afraid. Am I in the place of God? You intended to harm me, but God intended it for good to accomplish what is now being done, the saving of many lives. So then, don't be afraid. I will provide for you and your children." And he reassured them and spoke kindly to them.

CHARACTER CHECK

How is God working out his plans for me through my disappointments?

_____

_____

_____

_____

_____

IN BUSINESS TERMS

Harlan Sanders' career amounted to a string of failures.

He failed as a blacksmith. He got fired as a railroad locomotive fireman with the Southern Railroad. He tried selling insurance, studying law, selling tires, running a filling station, and even running a ferryboat. Nothing worked out. Later in life, he became chief cook and bottlewasher at a restaurant.

When Sanders got his first Social Security check–only $105–he became angry. But Sanders took that first check and started a business: Kentucky Fried Chicken. The rest, as they say, is history.

Sometimes God prepares us for success through the hard knocks of life. We may dislike the process, but God builds character through disappointments and failures. So it was with Joseph. Not until later in life could he look back and admit that God intended the evil betrayal by his brothers, which landed him in Egypt, for good. Even while in Egypt, Joseph got a raw deal–he was falsely accused of trying to seduce the wife of a leading Egyptian government official! God worked through Joseph's circumstances later in life to make him the second in command in Egypt.

What God did for Joseph, God will do for us. The God of the universe is actively at work in our disappointments. He intends them for our good.

–Steven D. Mathewson

SOMETHING TO THINK ABOUT

Disappointment is often the salt of life.

—

Theodore Parker

AVOIDING BURNOUT

WHEN YOU'RE SWAMPED, THE TEMPTATION IS TO WORK HARDER. IN THE OLD TESTAMENT, AFTER THE EXODUS, MOSES WORKED HARD. TOO HARD. IT TOOK A WISE MAN LIKE HIS FATHER-IN-LAW, JETHRO, TO POINT THIS OUT. JETHRO OFFERED MOSES A STRATEGY FOR MAXIMIZING HIS PRODUCTIVITY WHILE CUTTING DOWN ON HIS WORKLOAD.

EXODUS 18:17–22

Moses' father-in-law replied, "What you are doing is not good. You and these people who come to you will only wear yourselves out. The work is too heavy for you; you cannot handle it alone. Listen now to me and I will give you some advice, and may God be with you. You must be the people's representative before God and bring their disputes to him. Teach them the decrees and laws, and show them the way to live and the duties they are to perform. But select capable men from all the people—men who fear God, trustworthy men who hate dishonest gain—and appoint them as officials over thousands, hundreds, fifties and tens. Have them serve as judges for the people at all times, but have them bring every difficult case to you; the simple cases they can decide themselves. That will make your load lighter, because they will share it with you."

CHARACTER CHECK
In my leadership roles, am I doing what only I can do?

_____

_____

_____

_____

_____

IN BUSINESS TERMS

Jethro suggested to his son-in-law Moses that he work smarter, not harder. When Jethro saw that Moses was on the brink of burnout, Jethro acted as a consultant and passed on a workable strategy. He first counseled Moses to concentrate on working in his area of strength. For Moses, that meant he needed to focus on his teaching and mentoring role.

Next, Jethro counseled Moses to build a capable team to handle most of the day-to-day decisions and duties. Jethro advised Moses to deal with only those issues that required his expertise. If someone else could handle it, someone else should do it.

A friend of mine invented a machine that cleans computer hard drives. Then, as CEO of his high-tech company, his workload grew to crushing proportions. As a result, Eric was forced to make some hard decisions. He chose to concentrate his time in an area in which he is most skilled—research and development. The process was painful at times, but the restructuring freed him up to do what he does best.

Such decisions require strong leadership. But God is honored, the leader does what only he or she can do, and people end up better served.

–Steven D. Mathewson

REST AND REFRESHMENT

PROFESSIONAL BASEBALL PITCHERS ARE USUALLY GIVEN AT LEAST THREE DAYS OF REST BETWEEN GAMES. THAT GIVES THEIR ARMS TIME TO RECOVER FROM THE STRESS OF PITCHING 90-MILE-AN-HOUR FAST BALLS FOR A COUPLE OF HOURS. WE, TOO, NEED A REGULAR BREAK FROM THE STRESS OF OUR LIVES. GOD HAS CALLED HIS PEOPLE TO SHUT DOWN FOR A DAY. WORK SIX DAYS; THEN REST ONE.

EXODUS 20:8–11; 23:12

"Remember the Sabbath day by keeping it holy. Six days you shall labor and do all your work, but the seventh day is a Sabbath to the LORD your God. On it you shall not do any work, neither you, nor your son or daughter, nor your manservant or maidservant, nor your animals, nor the alien within your gates. For in six days the LORD made the heavens and the earth, the sea, and all that is in them, but he rested on the seventh day. Therefore the LORD blessed the Sabbath day and made it holy. . . .

"Six days do your work, but on the seventh day do not work, so that your ox and your donkey may rest and the slave born in your household, and the alien as well, may be refreshed."

CHARACTER CHECK
What one change in my lifestyle could increase my delight in God?

_____

_____

_____

_____

_____

IN BUSINESS TERMS

Work must be regularly balanced with plenty of play. This isn't easy. Work–especially when it's satisfying–dons the regal robes of Importance and tyrannizes everything else. Play seems too small a thing to approach the throne with a request for time.

Perhaps this is why God commanded at least one day of play out of seven. It takes the hard edge of a commandment to cut back the ever-expanding encroachments of work. A divine suggestion wouldn't have stood a chance.

The Bible calls for a Sabbath rest, not a Sabbath play. But what is rest? I don't think it comes from doing nothing. I suggest we think of Sabbath rest as a time of God-ordained play. Play has two elements–freedom and delight. We play when, freed from the necessity of work, we do something for the sheer joy of it.

The center of Christian play is worship. What is praise but delight in God? Having been set free by grace, we enjoy the presence of God, playing as children with a Father in a holy game of love. With worship at the heart of play and play at the heart of worship, all play is lifted in importance. We may not demean this gift. To build a model train layout, to fly a glider or scuba dive–to do these things for no other reason than pure delight–is to do something holy, something that witnesses to the Sabbath rest we have in Christ.

–Donald McCullough

LAST WORDS

WHEN A CEO RETIRES, HE OR SHE OFTEN USES THE OCCASION TO MAKE A SPEECH THAT CHALLENGES THE HEARERS ABOUT THE FUTURE. SO IT WAS WITH THE OLD TESTAMENT LEADER JOSHUA IN THIS FAMOUS PASSAGE. "I AM ABOUT TO GO THE WAY OF ALL THE EARTH," HE TOLD HIS FOLLOWERS. THEN HE CHALLENGED THEM TO CHOOSE GOD.

JOSHUA 24:14–15, 23–24

"Now fear the LORD and serve him with all faithfulness. Throw away the gods your forefathers worshiped beyond the River and in Egypt, and serve the LORD. But if serving the LORD seems undesirable to you, then choose for yourselves this day whom you will serve, whether the gods your forefathers served beyond the River, or the gods of the Amorites, in whose land you are living. But as for me and my household, we will serve the LORD."

"Now then," said Joshua, "throw away the foreign gods that are among you and yield your hearts to the LORD, the God of Israel." And the people said to Joshua, "We will serve the LORD our God and obey him."

CHARACTER CHECK
How do my current priorities line up with what I say is important?

_____

_____

_____

_____

_____

IN BUSINESS TERMS

My most difficult decision was to quit accepting speaking engagements, regardless of how influential or interesting the setting. I reached this decision in 1977 after I began to feel that I was not at home with my family as much as I should be.

I had never abandoned my wife and children, but most speaking commitments occur on weekends–prime family time. I began to agonize over the contradiction: The Lord had given me a message about the family I wanted to convey, but how could I do it without sacrificing mine?

The dilemma continued for more than a year. Finally, a day came when a decision had to be made. Auditoriums had to be scheduled for the following year, and the booking deadline had arrived. One evening, we prayed together as a family and asked the Lord to make the decision for us. Then we went to bed. Shirley and I decided to read for a while. I picked up a book, and after about twenty pages, I came across a reference to the eighteenth chapter of Exodus, where Moses is visited by his father-in-law, Jethro, who is concerned because Moses was accepting too many responsibilities. As I read the first verse, the Lord seemed to say, "This is your answer."

–James Dobson

SOMETHING TO THINK ABOUT

Think of only three things—God, your family, and the Green Bay Packers— in that order.

—

Vince Lombardi

NEED TO BE NEEDED

MOST WHO SCALE THE CORPORATE LADDER QUICKLY DO WELL AT TWO THINGS: MAN-
AGING MONEY AND MANAGING PEOPLE. THE MORE DIFFICULT CHALLENGE IS MANAG-
ING PEOPLE. ONE REASON IS OUR PROPENSITY TO WANT TO BE LIKED. BUT THE
AFFECTIONS OF OTHERS ARE FICKLE. IN THE OLD TESTAMENT, DAVID FOUND OUT
THAT EVEN THOSE HE COUNTED ON TURNED AGAINST HIM.

1 SAMUEL 30:1–6

*David and his men reached Ziklag on the third day. Now the
Amalekites had raided the Negev and Ziklag. They had attacked Ziklag
and burned it, and had taken captive the women and all who were in it,
both young and old. They killed none of them, but carried them off as
they went on their way.*

*When David and his men came to Ziklag, they found it destroyed
by fire and their wives and sons and daughters taken captive. So David
and his men wept aloud until they had no strength left to weep. David's
two wives had been captured—Ahinoam of Jezreel and Abigail, the
widow of Nabal of Carmel. David was greatly distressed because the men
were talking of stoning him; each one was bitter in spirit because of his
sons and daughters. But David found strength in the LORD his God.*

CHARACTER CHECK
Why do I need to be liked?

_____

_____

_____

_____

_____

IN BUSINESS TERMS

I came from a home in which my mother divorced seven times and was an alcoholic. I didn't fully realize the impact my background had on me, but one afternoon about 4 p.m., I found myself sitting at my desk completely immobilized. I had been helping one person after another in an effort to gain their approval. I had lost all sense of my own boundaries.

There I sat, unable to move, unable to talk, and all I could do was cry.

It was as if the Lord spoke to me, saying, "Ted, why have you always had to be a cut above others? You weren't content to be a pilot; you had to be a Marine fighter pilot. If others showed off by flying under a bridge, you had to fly under a bridge upside down. You weren't satisfied with a college degree; you had to have a doctor's degree. Why?"

In that moment I broke down. I realized how my need for approval was destroying my life and ministry. That experience was one of the best things that happened to me.

I've now rediscovered what I once knew as a boy. When my stepfather would beat my mother, I would leave the house with my dog and my rifle, go into the hills, and stay there for a few days. I would talk to God with childlike innocence and trust and listen for what the Lord had to say.

Now I see success as being in touch with the voice of God.

–Ted Roberts

_____

_____

_____

_____

_____

ROAD OUT OF DISCONTENTMENT

MIDLIFE FOR MOST PEOPLE PROMPTS A NEED TO REFLECT AND REEVALUATE. THAT TIME IN LIFE CAN CREATE A BASIC DISSATISFACTION WITH LIFE—AND GOD. AND THUS CREATE OTHER TROUBLES. WHY DID KING DAVID, THE "MAN AFTER GOD'S OWN HEART," COMMIT SUCH A GRIEVOUS SIN AS ADULTERY? GOD PINPOINTED THAT DAVID WAS NOT CONTENT WITH WHAT GOD HAD GIVEN HIM.

2 SAMUEL 12:7–10

Then Nathan said to David, "You are the man! This is what the LORD, the God of Israel, says: 'I anointed you king over Israel, and I delivered you from the hand of Saul. I gave your master's house to you, and your master's wives into your arms. I gave you the house of Israel and Judah. And if all this had been too little, I would have given you even more.

"'Why did you despise the word of the LORD by doing what is evil in his eyes? You struck down Uriah the Hittite with the sword and took his wife to be your own. You killed him with the sword of the Ammonites. Now, therefore, the sword shall never depart from your house, because you despised me and took the wife of Uriah the Hittite to be your own.'"

CHARACTER CHECK

In what area of life do I feel dissatisfied? Why?

_____

_____

_____

_____

_____

IN BUSINESS TERMS

Most adulterous situations are not primarily the result of a sexual problem.

I've observed that sexual problems are life problems. That is, when you really get down to the bottom of why something happened, it's rarely just sexual dissatisfaction with a spouse or lustful desire for the other person. Almost every individual I've seen has been dealing with some form of impotence–not sexual impotence necessarily, but what we might call "life impotence."

People are most vulnerable to sexual temptation, I've found, when they're unable to achieve their goals, when they're frustrated or they're discouraged, when their dreams are being dashed. The sexual involvement grows out of feeling that their lives are out of control, that they're personally impotent. Life is not affirming their value as people.

Then along comes a person who does affirm the hurting person's value, who accepts him just as he is, who indicates she finds him very attractive.

–Jay Kesler

SOMETHING TO THINK ABOUT

Contrary to popular opinion, sin is not what you want to do but can't; it is what you should not do because it will hurt you—and hurt you bad.

—

Steve Brown

SUCCESS AT HOME

KING DAVID KNEW THE PAIN OF A WAYWARD SON. ALL OF HIS ACCOMPLISHMENTS AS A WARRIOR, A POET, A MUSICIAN, AND A KING COULD NOT OFFSET THE GRIEF HE FELT WHEN HE RECEIVED WORD OF HIS SON ABSALOM'S DEATH.

2 SAMUEL 18:24, 31–33

While David was sitting between the inner and outer gates, the watchman went up to the roof of the gateway by the wall. As he looked out, he saw a man running alone. . . .

Then the Cushite arrived and said, "My lord the king, hear the good news! The LORD has delivered you today from all who rose up against you."

The king asked the Cushite, "Is the young man Absalom safe?"

The Cushite replied, "May the enemies of my lord the king and all who rise up to harm you be like that young man."

The king was shaken. He went up to the room over the gateway and wept. As he went, he said: "O my son Absalom! My son, my son Absalom! If only I had died instead of you–O Absalom, my son, my son!"

CHARACTER CHECK
What kind of legacy am I passing on to my children?

_____

_____

_____

_____

_____

IN BUSINESS TERMS

During my childhood, my father served as executive director of a Christian organization. I can't count the number of times we dropped him off or picked him up at the Peoria (Illinois) airport. My brothers and I shared in the sacrifice of my dad's leadership role. But he never sacrificed his.

In fact, he poured as much time into shaping us and spending time with us as he did with his ministry. One way he did this was by modeling a passion outside his work. I can think of two: cars and hunting.

A few miles from my hometown, Lawrence Fogleberg directed a high school band. In fact, he was occasionally a judge when our band would go to district competitions, or he would direct local festivals. His son Dan, now a popular folk singer, wrote a beautiful tribute to his dad, the "Leader of the Band." He sings of how, though the leader of the band may be getting tired, "his blood runs through my instrument, and his heart is in my soul."

That's how I feel about my dad and mom. They gave me a gift I know I never can repay. I'm a living legacy of their love and ministry. I hope my children can say the same about me.

–Steve Mathewson

SOMETHING
TO THINK
ABOUT
Families are God's primary missionary society.

—

Lewis Smedes

INTEGRITY IS EVERYTHING

CHARACTER ALWAYS TRUMPS THE BOTTOM LINE. FIRST KINGS 9 RECORDS GOD'S APPEARANCE TO KING SOLOMON AFTER HE COMPLETED THE HUGE PROJECT OF BUILDING GOD'S TEMPLE. GOD STRESSED THE NEED FOR SOLOMON TO WALK IN INTEGRITY. HIS FUTURE SUCCESS WOULD HINGE ON IT.

1 KINGS 9:3–7

The Lord said to him:

"I have heard the prayer and plea you have made before me; I have consecrated this temple, which you have built, by putting my Name there forever. My eyes and my heart will always be there.

"As for you, if you walk before me in integrity of heart and uprightness, as David your father did, and do all I command and observe my decrees and laws, I will establish your royal throne over Israel forever, as I promised David your father' . . .

"But if you or your sons turn away from me and do not observe the commands and decrees I have given you and go off to serve other gods and worship them, then I will cut off Israel from the land I have given them and will reject this temple I have consecrated for my Name. Israel will then become a byword and an object of ridicule among all peoples."

CHARACTER CHECK

In which areas of my life do I have integrity? In which areas do I lack it?

IN BUSINESS TERMS

It cost me a lot of money in a bad investment to learn that in leadership, character is more important than intelligence. I had mistakenly put intelligence above character. Intelligence is important, but character is more important. One of America's wealthiest investors said at Harvard that the three qualities he looks for in those in whom he will invest are character, intelligence, and energy.

Character is so important because it cannot be fully evaluated but will fail at the time when we can least afford it. It is almost impossible to buttress weak character.

My experience has brought me to a controversial belief about character: Character is sectionalized like a grapefruit, not homogeneous like a bottle of milk. When we say a person has a strong character or weak character, we assume that his character is of one piece of cloth. I have not found this true. Some people who are totally honest in business are hypocritical in personal life. Some are trustworthy in one section of their life and untrustworthy in another. I've always been intrigued by the story that Willie Sutton, the bank robber, cried when he had to lie to his mother about where he was.

–Fred Smith

BEFORE YOU QUIT

WHEN YOU HIT THE WALL AT WORK OR IN LIFE, GOD SOMETIMES SHOWS HIS PRESENCE IN UNEXPECTED WAYS. TAKE THE OLD TESTAMENT PROPHET ELIJAH, FOR EXAMPLE. IN THE AFTERMATH OF HIS SHOWDOWN WITH THE PROPHETS OF BAAL, ELIJAH FEARED THAT HIS MINISTRY HAD FAILED AND WANTED TO QUIT. GOD GENTLY INSTRUCTED ELIJAH TO "GO BACK THE WAY YOU CAME" AND TAKE UP HIS WORK AGAIN.

1 KINGS 19:9b–13, 15

And the word of the Lord came to him: "What are you doing here, Elijah?"

He replied, "I have been very zealous for the Lord God Almighty. The Israelites have rejected your covenant, broken down your altars, and put your prophets to death with the sword. I am the only one left, and now they are trying to kill me too."

"The Lord said, "Go out and stand on the mountain in the presence of the Lord, for the Lord is about to pass by."

Then a great and powerful wind tore the mountains apart and shattered the rocks before the Lord, but the Lord was not in the wind. After the wind there was an earthquake, but the Lord was not in the earthquake. After the earthquake came a fire, but the Lord was not in the fire. And after the fire came a gentle whisper. When Elijah heard it, he pulled his cloak over his face . . .

The Lord said to him, "Go back the way you came. . . ."

CHARACTER CHECK

When I feel like throwing in the towel, what keeps me going?

_____

_____

_____

_____

_____

IN BUSINESS TERMS

Last spring, toward the end of the school year, I got a call on Sunday morning: "Dr. Willimon, there's no electricity in the chapel this morning."

"Has the choir gotten in?" I asked.

"I think so. I can hear people moving around, but it's so dark I can't see anyone."

I hurried over to do what I could. We stuck lit candles all over the place. The organ wouldn't work. The PA system was down. Nothing went right, and I ran around for two hours improvising and calming upset people. At ten minutes before the service, the lights came on, but I felt awful–unprepared, disheveled, angry. I staggered through the service, thinking to myself, *I hate this place!*

But as I was greeting people leaving the church, three undergraduate women I didn't know came up and said, "Dr. Willimon, we're all graduating this year, and we were just talking about how some of our best memories will be the services we've had here in the chapel. We just wanted to thank you."

I said, "Did God send you here today?"

My reaction afterward was almost a sort of disgust. I thought, *That's typical of God: you get finally to the point that you're ready to throw in the towel because it's all so absurd, and then God sends you three girls with a message like that!* So I decided to stick with the ministry another week.

–William Willimon

TRUE TO GOD

WISE INVESTORS ALWAYS TAKE THE LONG VIEW—THAT OVER TIME, THE STOCK MAR-
KET WILL RISE. THEY STICK TO THEIR PLAN EVEN WHEN A BEAR MARKET ERODES THE
VALUE OF THEIR PORTFOLIO. THE SAME HOLDS TRUE FOR THE PERSON WHO REFUSES
TO COMPROMISE WHEN LIFE GETS DIFFICULT. KING JOSIAH DREW A LINE IN THE
SAND—HE AND HIS PEOPLE WOULD FOLLOW GOD.

2 CHRONICLES 34:29–33

*Then the king called together all the elders of Judah and Jerusalem. He
went up to the temple of the LORD with the men of Judah, the people of
Jerusalem, the priests and the Levites–all the people from the least to the
greatest. He read in their hearing all the words of the Book of the Covenant,
which had been found in the temple of the LORD. The king stood by his pil-
lar and renewed the covenant in the presence of the LORD–to follow the
LORD and keep his commands, regulations and decrees with all his heart
and all his soul, and to obey the words of the covenant written in this book.*

*Then he had everyone in Jerusalem and Benjamin pledge them-
selves to it; the people of Jerusalem did this in accordance with the
covenant of God, the God of their fathers. . . . As long as he lived, they
did not fail to follow the LORD, the God of their fathers.*

CHARACTER CHECK
Settle that you are going to follow Christ no matter what the repercussions are.

_____

_____

_____

_____

_____

IN BUSINESS TERMS

In his newspaper column "Market Report," Bill Barnhart explained the difference between investors and traders. "A trader in a stock," wrote Barnhart, "is making decisions minute-by-minute in the hope of shaving off profits measured in fractions of a dollar. An investor, on the other hand, typically buys or sells a stock based on views about the company and the economy at large."

In other words, traders pursue short-term profits. By contrast, investors are in it for the long haul. They commit their money to a stock, believing that over years the stock will grow in value. Investors aren't flustered by the ups and downs of the market because they believe in the quality of the company.

In the kingdom of God, there are also investors and traders. They come to Christ with very different goals. Traders in the kingdom want God to improve their lot in this world. If following Christ means pain or hardship, they sell out.

But investors in the kingdom stay true to Christ no matter what happens in this world, knowing that eternal dividends await them.

–Craig Brian Larson

THE RIGHT QUESTION

WHEN MICROSOFT LAUNCHED WINDOWS 95, THE ADVERTISING SLOGAN ASKED, "WHERE DO YOU WANT TO GO TODAY?" WHILE THAT WORKED FOR SELLING WINDOWS 95, IT IS THE WRONG QUESTION FOR SPIRITUAL PROGRESS. THE STORY OF NEHEMIAH IN THE OLD TESTAMENT POINTS US TO ANOTHER QUESTION: WHERE DOES GOD WANT TO TAKE ME?

NEHEMIAH 2:4–5, 7–8, 12B

The king said to me, "What is it you want?"

Then I prayed to the God of heaven, and I answered the king, "If it pleases the king and if your servant has found favor in his sight, let him send me to the city in Judah where my fathers are buried so that I can rebuild it." . . .

I also said to him, "If it pleases the king, may I have letters to the governors of Trans-Euphrates, so that they will provide me safe-conduct until I arrive in Judah? And may I have a letter to Asaph, keeper of the king's forest, so he will give me timber to make beams for the gates of the citadel by the temple and for the city wall and for the residence I will occupy?" . . .

I had not told anyone what my God had put in my heart to do for Jerusalem.

CHARACTER CHECK
Where does Christ want to take me? How do I discern his direction?

_____

_____

_____

_____

_____

IN BUSINESS TERMS

Vision arises out of our burden to know the will of God, to become whatever it is God wants us to become. Vision is the product of God working in us. He creates the vision, and we receive it. Goal setting is the projection of our perceptions of what we want to accomplish. There's nothing particularly nefarious about that–it's just that vision is something that elicits a response from us, that calls us forth. Goals, on the other hand, are things we project.

That is why I suppose I'm not as firmly committed to goals– I (or we) thought them up in the first place. Vision, on the other hand, *summons* me.

The process of goal setting cannot be bad. But if the church is indeed an organism and I am part of the body of Christ, it's not really a matter of "Where do I want to go?" but rather "Where does Christ want to take me?"

–Terry Fullam

VISION INTO REALITY

MOST ENTREPRENEURS ARE VISIONARIES; THEY SEE THE FUTURE AND THEN TAKE GREAT RISKS TO CREATE IT. IN THE OLD TESTAMENT, NEHEMIAH WAS A GREAT VISIONARY. BUT HE WAS ALSO A MAN OF ACTION. HIS MASTER PLAN DIDN'T SIT ON HIS DESK COLLECTING DUST. HIS GOALS WERE NOT MERELY THEORETICAL. THE WORK GOT DONE.

NEHEMIAH 2:17–18; 3:1–2

Then I said to them, "You see the trouble we are in: Jerusalem lies in ruins, and its gates have been burned with fire. Come, let us rebuild the wall of Jerusalem, and we will no longer be in disgrace." I also told them about the gracious hand of my God upon me and what the king had said to me. . . .

Eliashib the high priest and his fellow priests went to work and rebuilt the Sheep Gate. They dedicated it and set its doors in place, building as far as the Tower of the Hundred, which they dedicated, and as far as the Tower of Hananel. The men of Jericho built the adjoining section, and Zaccur son of Imri built next to them.

CHARACTER CHECK
What tough decision that I've put off do I need to make?

_____

_____

_____

_____

_____

IN BUSINESS TERMS

As I stepped off the plane, the pastor and the chairman of the long-range planning committee met me. As we were waiting on my luggage, they gave me three notebooks thick with data, which they had invested two years in gathering. They asked me if I would look at them before the 7:30 breakfast the next morning.

When we gathered for breakfast, they asked me, "What do you think?"

"Good friends," I said, "the day for analysis is over. The day for action has arrived."

If you had a bar graph to determine the level of certainty for their decision, it would have read 65 percent. They'd spent two years and gathered three notebooks of data because they believed the more data they gathered, the more they could raise the level of certainty–perhaps to 85 or 90 percent.

There are a lot of decisions in life we have to make with a 65 percent level of certainty.

I said, "Even with seven notebooks of data, the level of certainty for the decision is still going to be about 65 percent. So let us decide."

–Kennon Callahan

SOMETHING TO THINK ABOUT

He who deliberates fully before taking a step will spend his entire life on one leg.

—

Chinese proverb

WHERE INTEGRITY BEGINS

PSALM 15 RAISES A QUESTION ABOUT WHAT KIND OF PEOPLE ARE FIT TO COME
INTO GOD'S PRESENCE TO WORSHIP HIM. PEOPLE FIT TO WORSHIP GOD PRACTICE
INTEGRITY IN THEIR SPEECH, IN THEIR RELATIONSHIPS WITH NEIGHBORS, IN THEIR
BUSINESS DEALINGS, AND IN THEIR FINANCIAL TRANSACTIONS. THE EVERYDAY ROU-
TINE EXPOSES OUR INTEGRITY OR LACK OF IT.

PSALM 15

LORD, *who may dwell in your sanctuary? Who may live on your
holy hill?*

*He whose walk is blameless and who does what is righteous, who
speaks the truth from his heart and has no slander on his tongue, who
does his neighbor no wrong and casts no slur on his fellowman, who
despises a vile man but honors those who fear the LORD, who keeps his
oath even when it hurts, who lends his money without usury and does
not accept a bribe against the innocent.*

He who does these things will never be shaken.

CHARACTER CHECK
What is troubling me in the middle of the night? What might God be saying?

_____

_____

_____

_____

_____

IN BUSINESS TERMS

After speaking to a group of corporate officers, several of us gathered around for a bull session. One of the CEOs, with his tongue loosened by spirits from the bottle, said, "Fred, you talk a lot about self-respect. How do you define it?"

I said, "Bill, I can't give you a dictionary definition, but I can tell you how I know I've got it. When I wake up at three o'clock in the morning, I talk to the little guy inside me who is still simple, honest, and knows right from wrong. He hasn't rationalized enough to become sophisticated. He still sees things black and white. He is the 'honest me.' When we can talk freely, I know we respect who I am. When he turns away and won't talk freely, I know I'm in trouble. If he says, 'Get lost; you're a phony,' I know that I've lost my self-respect."

Instantly the CEO jumped out of his chair, circled it, and said, "Man, you've done plowed up a snake!"

Evidently his night dialogues were troubling him. A few months later I understood his response better when I read he was under investigation.

–Fred Smith, Sr.

SOMETHING TO THINK ABOUT

He is rich or poor according to what he is, not according to what he has.

—

Henry Ward Beecher

CHOOSING DELIGHT

MANY PROFESSIONALS, ESPECIALLY AT MIDLIFE, WONDER WHETHER THEY'RE REALLY WHERE GOD WANTS THEM TO BE. MANY GRIT THEIR TEETH AND SOLDIER ON, WHILE DOUBTS NAG THEM FOR YEARS. SOME NEVER MAKE THE CHANGES NECESSARY TO FIND A NEW DIRECTION. KING DAVID UNDERSTOOD THAT GOD'S WILL WAS NOT FOR HIS CHILD TO BE MISERABLE.

PSALM 16:5–11

LORD, you have assigned me my portion and my cup; you have made my lot secure. The boundary lines have fallen for me in pleasant places; surely I have a delightful inheritance.

I will praise the LORD, who counsels me; even at night my heart instructs me. I have set the LORD always before me. Because he is at my right hand, I will not be shaken.

Therefore my heart is glad and my tongue rejoices; my body also will rest secure, because you will not abandon me to the grave, nor will you let your Holy One see decay. You have made known to me the path of life; you will fill me with joy in your presence, with eternal pleasures at your right hand.

CHARACTER CHECK
What prevents me from taking the risk to do what I really love to do?

_____

_____

_____

_____

_____

IN BUSINESS TERMS

It's important that you look at the gifts God has given you. You need to inventory your gifts so you can be a good steward. Then ask, Where does God move my heart to use these gifts? And with what circumstances, what particular kinds of problems, what groups of people? People find they have many more gifts than they supposed.

There are many opportunities to do ministry in the world God has made rather than only those within the church God has made. Isn't that what John Wesley did? He went to the coal miners and to the marginalized people outside the institutional church.

Too strong a view of the fallen nature of man causes us to assume that what we delight to do is probably a sin. If a non-Christian doesn't enjoy selling manure, he naturally thinks, *Maybe I should get into something else.* But Christians tend to say, "God must have put me here for some reason." So they end up baptizing inertia.

I don't think inertia necessarily is divine. Rest–inertia–is supposed to be a part of the rhythm of life, not the definition of life.

–Richard Nelson Bolles

JOY FROM GOD'S PRESENCE

JOY IS WHAT YOU FEEL WHEN YOU'VE JUST LANDED THE JOB OF YOUR DREAMS. JOY INSPIRES YOU TO BURST INTO SONG. IN THE OLD TESTAMENT, KING DAVID WAS MOVED TO JOY BY THE VICTORIES AND RICH BLESSINGS PROVIDED BY GOD. IN FACT, EXPERIENCING THE PRESENCE OF GOD BROUGHT JOY TO DAVID'S LIFE. IN RESPONSE, DAVID PENNED PSALM 21.

PSALM 21:1–7

O LORD, the king rejoices in your strength. How great is his joy in the victories you give! You have granted him the desire of his heart and have not withheld the request of his lips. Selah

You welcomed him with rich blessings and placed a crown of pure gold on his head. He asked you for life, and you gave it to him—length of days, for ever and ever. Through the victories you gave, his glory is great; you have bestowed on him splendor and majesty. Surely you have granted him eternal blessings and made him glad with the joy of your presence. For the king trusts in the LORD; through the unfailing love of the Most High he will not be shaken.

CHARACTER CHECK
Is my capacity for experiencing God in worship increasing?

_____

_____

_____

_____

_____

IN BUSINESS TERMS

When I was a pastor in New Jersey, a black pastor-friend invited me to preach at his church in Jamaica, Queens. The place was rocking. I was up front on the platform clapping my hands when Rod leaned over to me and said, "You know why those people are all smiling at you, don't you?" I said no.

"They're laughing at you 'cause you don't know how to move."

There's an ecstatic dimension of joy, which is to let yourself be moved. The word *ecstasy* means "to be moved out of your place." Joy is the capacity to be moved, to be shifted, to be taken out of something. I want to be able to move, in a literal sense.

You can fall into the trap of trying to manufacture sensational experiences in worship, but I don't think we can have joy until we're willing to let ourselves be moved, shifted.

–Ben Patterson

SOMETHING
TO THINK
ABOUT
Joy is almost never in our power, and pleasure often is.

—

C. S. Lewis

GOD OF REST

PSALM 23 IS OFTEN READ AT FUNERALS, BUT IT ALSO HAS SOMETHING TO SAY TO THE OVERCOMMITTED. THIS PSALM REMINDS US THAT GOD IS NOT A SLAVEDRIVER WHO WANTS US TO SQUEEZE OUT EVERY MINUTE OF THE DAY FOR ACTIVITY. HE IS A GOD WHO BRINGS REST AND SERENITY TO OUR LIVES.

PSALM 23

The LORD is my shepherd, I shall not be in want.

He makes me lie down in green pastures, he leads me beside quiet waters, he restores my soul. He guides me in paths of righteousness for his name's sake. Even though I walk through the valley of the shadow of death, I will fear no evil, for you are with me; your rod and your staff, they comfort me.

You prepare a table before me in the presence of my enemies. You anoint my head with oil; my cup overflows. Surely goodness and love will follow me all the days of my life, and I will dwell in the house of the LORD forever.

CHARACTER CHECK
How does my view of God contribute to my work habits?

_____

_____

_____

_____

_____

IN BUSINESS TERMS

I have friends who are professional rodeo cowboys. In their quest to make the National Finals each year, they push themselves to compete in more than a hundred rodeos over ten months, often driving all night to get to the next one.

As one said to me a few years ago, "It's not the bulls that will wear you down, it's seeing too many sunrises through the windshield of a pickup." Like other professional athletes, most rodeo cowboys see their careers end sometime around their thirtieth birthday.

A thousand times while growing up, I heard my parents or grandparents yawn, stretch, and say, "There's no rest for the wicked." To which the conditioned response was always, "And the righteous don't need any."

But just as chronic fatigue will kill sexual passion, it can stifle spiritual passion. Worse, fatigue makes maintaining intimacy with God almost impossible. Passion dies. In its place is either a void or a hastily constructed, unconvincing facsimile of the real thing.

–Ed Rowell

SOMETHING TO THINK ABOUT

Perpetual devotion to what a man calls his business is only to be sustained by perpetual neglect of many other things.

—

Robert Louis Stevenson

CONFESSION MODEL

WHEN WAS THE LAST TIME YOU HEARD SOMEONE IN A MEETING SAY, "THAT WAS MY RESPONSIBILITY. I DROPPED THE BALL." KING DAVID WAS A GREAT SINNER, BUT HE WAS ALSO A GREAT CONFESSOR. HE OWNED UP TO HIS SIN. PSALM 32 OFFERS BELIEVERS A MODEL FOR CONFESSION.

PSALM 32:1–5

Blessed is he whose transgressions are forgiven, whose sins are covered. Blessed is the man whose sin the LORD does not count against him and in whose spirit is no deceit.

When I kept silent, my bones wasted away through my groaning all day long. For day and night your hand was heavy upon me; my strength was sapped as in the heat of summer. Selah

Then I acknowledged my sin to you and did not cover up my iniquity. I said, "I will confess my transgressions to the LORD"–and you forgave the guilt of my sin. Selah

CHARACTER CHECK
Allow God to search your heart today.

_____

_____

_____

_____

_____

IN BUSINESS TERMS

[Unless I make an effort to confess my sins to God,] I can muddle on in my interaction with him for weeks, even years. John writes, "If we confess our sins, he is faithful and just to forgive us our sins, and to cleanse us from all unrighteousness" (1 John 1:9, KJV).

I've discovered that my fellowship with God is restored when my confession is specific. Each sin needs individual attention. Today my confession model is simple. When I realize I have sinned, I detail to God what I did and then say, "I agree with you that what I did was wrong." I ask God to forgive me and then affirm my intention never to commit that sin again. I pray on a regular basis the prayer in Psalm 139: "Search me, O God, and know my heart; test me and know my anxious thoughts. See if there is any offensive way in me, and lead me in the way everlasting" (vv. 23–24, NIV).

I wait quietly for God to bring unconfessed sin to my attention. The Holy Spirit is very specific: "At 4 P.M. last Tuesday, Roger, you did this and this and this."

–Roger Barrier

SOMETHING TO THINK ABOUT

I have more trouble with D. L. Moody than any other man I know.

—

D. L. Moody

WHEN LIFE GETS TOO HARD

PEOPLE WHO MAKE THINGS HAPPEN TEND TO RISE QUICKLY IN BUSINESS. THOSE SKILLS ARE VALUABLE AND GOD-GIVEN, BUT WHEN LIFE FALLS APART, THEY OFTEN DO US NO GOOD. PSALM 46 AFFIRMS THE SUFFICIENCY OF GOD'S MIGHTY PRESENCE WHEN LIFE GETS TOO BIG FOR US TO HANDLE. GOD GIVES HIS PEOPLE PERMISSION NOT TO FIX EVERYTHING.

PSALM 46:1–3, 7–11

God is our refuge and strength, an ever-present help in trouble. Therefore we will not fear, though the earth give way and the mountains fall into the heart of the sea, though its waters roar and foam and the mountains quake with their surging. . . .

The LORD Almighty is with us; the God of Jacob is our fortress. Selah. Come and see the works of the LORD, the desolations he has brought on the earth. He makes wars cease to the ends of the earth; he breaks the bow and shatters the spear, he burns the shields with fire. "Be still, and know that I am God; I will be exalted among the nations, I will be exalted in the earth."

The LORD Almighty is with us; the God of Jacob is our fortress. Selah.

CHARACTER CHECK
What one thing could I let go this week, trusting God to take care of it?

_____

_____

_____

_____

_____

IN BUSINESS TERMS

Most of us view success as fame, accomplishment, and acquisition. Our society has chosen personality over character. Christian success must be built of character, not of personality or skill. The great qualities in life are involved in the positive characteristics of a person, such as wisdom, integrity, honesty, loyalty, faith, forgiveness, and love.

The Everyday Bible gives an interesting translation of Psalm 131: "Lord, my heart is not proud. I do not look down on others. I do not do great things and I cannot do miracles. But I am calm and quiet."

How can we claim Christian success unless our hearts are calm and quiet? Thomas Kelly, the eminent Quaker philosopher, said that inside each person there should be a quiet center that nothing can disturb. The great Christian mystics continually talked of the throne of God, which is in the innermost part of our heart, where no storm, tribulation, or temptation can disturb.

Scripture says, "Greater is he who controls his spirit than he who takes a city." Obviously our condition is more than our accomplishment. Our greatest accomplishment is our condition.

–Fred Smith, Sr.

_____

_____

_____

_____

_____

TRUE IDENTITY

"I AM A LAWYER." "I SELL COMMODITIES." "I OWN A SMALL BUSINESS." IT'S SO
EASY TO BECOME WHAT WE DO. FREEDOM COMES, HOWEVER, WHEN WE REALIZE THAT
OUR CORE IDENTITY IS GOD IN JESUS CHRIST. IN THIS PSALM, KING DAVID
UNDERSCORES THAT IT IS "GOD ALONE" WHOM WE NEED. GOD ALONE IS OUR
SOURCE OF IDENTITY.

PSALM 62:1–2, 5–7

My soul finds rest in God alone;

my salvation comes from him.

He alone is my rock and my salvation;

he is my fortress, I will never be shaken. . . .

Find rest, O my soul, in God alone;

my hope comes from him.

He alone is my rock and my salvation;

he is my fortress, I will not be shaken.

My salvation and my honor depend on God;

he is my mighty rock, my refuge.

CHARACTER CHECK
Is my identity what I do?

_____

_____

_____

_____

_____

IN BUSINESS TERMS

If you're a banker, and you go to work today and your bank has just merged with another and they don't need you anymore, your identity has just been taken away from you without any say.

If your identity is being a husband, and your wife just fell in love with her tennis instructor and lets you know that she wants half and she's out the door, your identity is gone.

The question of who you are is one of those profound questions that even successful people have not necessarily answered. In fact, their discovery of identity is complicated by their success. The more successful you are in your field, the more you tend to be niched in most people's thinking.

I had a serious auto accident, and when neurologists looked at me, they said, "You're going to be fine. We just don't know whether you're going to have your mental edge and your memory."

I said, "Can I tell you what I do for a living? I stand for an hour in front of people every weekend trying to convince them that I'm one step ahead of them on the most important issues of life, and I do it from memory!"

What I had to deal with was, "Do I find my identity at work, or do I bring my identity to work?"

–Bob Shank

SOMETHING TO THINK ABOUT

Not only do we know God through Jesus Christ, we only know ourselves through Jesus Christ.

—

Blaise Pascal

WAITING FOR GOD

AT WORK, WE ALL WANT TO BE SOLUTIONS-ORIENTED. WHEN A PROBLEM ARISES, THE BEST AND THE BRIGHTEST DON'T WRING THEIR HANDS. THEY GET AFTER IT. THEY FIND ANSWERS. THEY COME UP WITH ALTERNATIVES. IN OUR SPIRITUAL LIFE, HOWEVER, SOMETIMES THERE ARE NO SOLUTIONS WE CAN PROVIDE. IN THIS PSALM, THE WRITER AGONIZES OVER NOT HEARING FROM GOD.

PSALM 77:1–3, 7–12

I cried out to God for help; I cried out to God to hear me. When I was in distress, I sought the Lord; at night I stretched out untiring hands and my soul refused to be comforted. I remembered you, O God, and I groaned; I mused, and my spirit grew faint. . . .

"Will the Lord reject forever? Will he never show his favor again? Has his unfailing love vanished forever? Has his promise failed for all time? Has God forgotten to be merciful? Has he in anger withheld his compassion?"

Then I thought, "To this I will appeal: the years of the right hand of the Most High." I will remember the deeds of the LORD; yes, I will remember your miracles of long ago. I will meditate on all your works and consider all your mighty deeds.

CHARACTER CHECK

Is my spiritual dryness my responsibility or God's?

_____

_____

_____

_____

_____

IN BUSINESS TERMS

From time to time, every Christian ends up hiking through a spiritual desert. Our sense of God wanes. Prayer and solitude and Bible reading seem to be a waste of effort.

For many, the tendency is to want to do something about the dryness. A friend recently said, "I just don't feel close to God like I used to. I haven't been spending enough time in prayer." His solution was more Bible reading and prayer–more effort. For some, spiritual dryness may be a signal of spiritual laziness, but that's not always the case. While God is always present with us, sometimes he withdraws from us the "sense" of His presence.

The great Christian writers down through the centuries have always written about spiritual dryness as though it were normal, part of what knowing God entails. Michael Molinos, a seventeenth-century Christian, wrote, "Dryness is good and holy, and cannot take you from the Divine presence. Do not call dryness a distraction."

The advice of the great cloud of Christian witnesses down through history is not to do more, but simply to keep hiking. Keep praying, keep listening for God, keep reading His Word, keep on keeping on–no matter how frustrated we feel.

The good news is the sense of God will eventually return, and by our faithfulness we make progress in our quest to know God.

–David L. Goetz

_____

_____

_____

_____

_____

GOD'S BIG TENT

WHILE DIVERSITY MAY BE A BUZZWORD, IT'S A FACT IN THE WORKPLACE. WHILE IT'S TEMPTING TO FEEL SUSPICIOUS OF THOSE WHO SEEM DIFFERENT, SUCH FEELINGS ARE AS OLD AS OLD TESTAMENT ISRAEL. WHEN AN ISRAELITE THOUGHT ABOUT AN EGYPTIAN OR A BABYLONIAN OR A PHILISTINE, HE OR SHE IMMEDIATELY THOUGHT ENEMY! BUT GOD'S PLAN INCLUDED PEOPLE FROM THOSE NATIONS.

PSALM 87

He has set his foundation on the holy mountain; the LORD loves the gates of Zion more than all the dwellings of Jacob.

Glorious things are said of you, O city of God:

"I will record Rahab and Babylon among those who acknowledge me—Philistia too, and Tyre, along with Cush—and will say, 'This one was born in Zion.'"

Indeed, of Zion it will be said, "This one and that one were born in her, and the Most High himself will establish her."

The LORD will write in the register of the peoples:

"This one was born in Zion. . . ."

As they make music they will sing, "All my fountains are in you."

CHARACTER CHECK

What prevents me from reaching out to those different from me?

_____

_____

_____

_____

_____

IN BUSINESS TERMS

The true enemy in our culture is relativism, not pluralism. There's actually nothing wrong with pluralism itself. It's simply a fact of life: our society contains differing backgrounds of faith and language. It is relativism, not pluralism, that calls the truth of the gospel into question. We don't need to fear pluralism. As the story of the early church demonstrates, the church has often prospered in pluralistic conditions.

Yet the church is having less and less impact on the culture, and the culture is having more and more impact on the church. The answer lies in letting the church be the church.

Christian disciples need to live out their callings, whether as doctors, lawyers, nurses, teachers, or whatever within their own sphere of influence. That will be far more effective than mounting a political campaign.

–Os Guinness

SOMETHING TO THINK ABOUT

If you're going to care about the fall of the sparrow you can't pick and choose who's going to be the sparrow.

—

Madeleine L'Engle

SEIZE THE DAY

WHEN YOU'RE GEARED TO THINK ABOUT THE FUTURE, YOU COME TO REALIZE HOW SHORT LIFE REALLY IS. THE OLD TESTAMENT LEADER MOSES CERTAINLY DID. IN PSALM 90, MOSES LAMENTS THE SHORTNESS OF LIFE. EVEN A LONG LIFE OF SEVENTY OR EIGHTY YEARS IS RELATIVELY SHORT. MOSES DECIDED TO CAPITALIZE ON THE OPPORTUNITY AFFORDED BY TIME.

PSALM 90:1–6, 9–10, 12

Lord, you have been our dwelling place throughout all generations. Before the mountains were born or you brought forth the earth and the world, from everlasting to everlasting you are God.

You turn men back to dust, saying, "Return to dust, O sons of men." For a thousand years in your sight are like a day that has just gone by, or like a watch in the night. You sweep men away in the sleep of death; they are like the new grass of the morning–though in the morning it springs up new, by evening it is dry and withered....

All our days pass away under your wrath; we finish our years with a moan. The length of our days is seventy years–or eighty, if we have the strength; yet their span is but trouble and sorrow, for they quickly pass, and we fly away.... Teach us to number our days aright, that we may gain a heart of wisdom.

CHARACTER CHECK
Do I have the right kind of busyness in my life?

_____

_____

_____

_____

_____

IN BUSINESS TERMS

A portion of Scripture that guides me constantly is 2 Peter 3:8, where Peter says, "To the Lord, a thousand years are as a day, and a day is as a thousand years."

I believe that every moment is an opportunity to be seized. Each day is as a thousand years; our twenty-four-hour slice of time is a sunrise-to-sunset opportunity for us to do something, by the grace of God, that counts for eternity, multiplying out to more than a thousand years.

I'm not saying that every moment, every day here equals a thousand years there. The proportions are what I think Peter was trying to get across: that this is how sacred, how valuable, how sanctified our moments really are.

A French mystic of the seventeenth century said that God does not give us time in which to do nothing. There is no such thing as empty time. Now, certainly there must be times of rest and respite, in which you go before the Lord in solitude. But even our meditation has a beautiful purpose–not utilitarian, in that it is something to be used–a sweet repose in which those moments of rest benefit the soul and end up glorifying God.

It makes our suffering purposeful. It doesn't mean you're any less busy–it may mean you're more busy. But the load is lightened knowing that this translates out to eternity–in your life, in another's life, and for the glory of God.
–Joni Eareckson Tada

_____

_____

_____

_____

_____

GOD'S CLAIM

LOYALTY IS THIN THESE DAYS IN THE PROFESSIONAL WORLD. BUT GOD PRACTICES LOYAL LOVE AND FAITHFULNESS TO HIS PEOPLE. PSALM 100, AFFECTIONATELY KNOWN AS THE "OLD ONE-HUNDREDTH," BURSTS WITH JOYFUL ENTHUSIASM. GOD CALLS US TO WORSHIP JOYFULLY WITH SHOUTS AND SONGS.

PSALM 100

Shout for joy to the LORD, all the earth.

Worship the LORD with gladness; come before him with joyful songs.

Know that the LORD is God. It is he who made us, and we are his; we are his people, the sheep of his pasture.

Enter his gates with thanksgiving and his courts with praise; give thanks to him and praise his name.

For the LORD is good and his love endures forever; his faithfulness continues through all generations.

CHARACTER CHECK

When was the last time you publicly gave thanks to God?

_____

_____

_____

_____

_____

IN BUSINESS TERMS

Biblical thanksgiving requires more than saying "thank you."

Most of the Old Testament was written in the Hebrew language. The Hebrew term *yadah* is often translated "give thanks" or "thanksgiving," but it actually means "to give public acknowledgment." If your friend, Bob, mows you're lawn while you're away, the American way to express thanksgiving is to go directly to Bob and say thank you. However, biblical thanksgiving goes public. It requires you to tell the community of worshipers about Bob's act of kindness.

Suppose God opens up the right house for you to purchase. Offers on two previous houses were rejected, but your offer on this latest house is accepted. You feel gratitude. This house will work out better than the first two at which you looked. It's in a better school district, and your payments will be lower. How should you respond to God as a worshiper? Certainly, it is appropriate to pray and thank God for providing the house. But you have not accomplished biblical thanksgiving until you go public. That requires telling other worshipers in a public setting how God provided for you. Biblical thanksgiving does not settle for anything less.

–Steve Mathewson

SOMETHING TO THINK ABOUT

Just the word *thanksgiving* prompts the spirit of humility. Genuine gratitude to God for His mercy, His abundance, His protection, His smile of favor. Life simplifies itself.

—

Charles Swindoll

WISDOM OF WAITING

WAITING SEEMS TO BE ABOUT 95 PERCENT OF LIFE. WAITING TO GET MARRIED.
WAITING TO HAVE A CHILD. WAITING FOR A JOB OFFER. CIRCUMSTANCES OFTEN
FORCE US TO LEARN THE WISDOM OF QUIETING OUR SOUL AND WAITING ON GOD.

PSALM 130

*Out of the depths I cry to you, O LORD; O Lord, hear my voice. Let
your ears be attentive to my cry for mercy.*

*If you, O LORD, kept a record of sins, O Lord, who could stand? But
with you there is forgiveness; therefore you are feared.*

*I wait for the LORD, my soul waits, and in his word I put my hope.
My soul waits for the Lord more than watchmen wait for the morning,
more than watchmen wait for the morning.*

*O Israel, put your hope in the LORD, for with the LORD is unfailing
love and with him is full redemption.*

He himself will redeem Israel from all their sins.

CHARACTER CHECK
What restless thoughts dominate my thinking? How can I give them to God?

_____

_____

_____

_____

_____

IN BUSINESS TERMS

We crowd our thoughts with so many agenda items that we don't take time to listen to God. God doesn't just talk to me at the end or at the beginning of a project, but all the time; he may have me change directions in the middle.

Now, I don't mean that you sit around waiting until God speaks in a burning bush. That may happen, but God also uses people to speak to you. Listen to them; stretch out your hand and let your people guide you.

Prayer is first of all listening to God. It's openness. God is always speaking; he's always doing something. Prayer is to enter into that activity. Take this room. Imagine you've never been out of it. Prayer is like going outside to see what's really there. Prayer in its most basic sense is just entering into an attitude of saying, "Lord, what are you saying to me?"

–Henri Nouwen

SOMETHING TO THINK ABOUT

In prayer it is better to have a heart without words than words without heart.

—

John Bunyan

HONEST INVENTORY

WHEN YOU BOOT UP A COMPUTER, IT OFTEN RAPIDLY GOES THROUGH A NUMBER OF SELF-TESTS TO MAKE SURE EVERYTHING IS WORKING PROPERLY. LEADERS, TOO, NEED TO GIVE THEMSELVES SELF-TESTS—HONEST, RIGOROUS INVENTORIES OF THEIR CHARACTER. KING DAVID RECOGNIZED THIS. IN PSALM 139 HE CELEBRATED GOD'S INTIMATE KNOWLEDGE OF EVEN THE SMALLEST DETAIL OF HIS LIFE.

PSALM 139:1–4, 23–24

O LORD, you have searched me and you know me.

You know when I sit and when I rise; you perceive my thoughts from afar.

You discern my going out and my lying down; you are familiar with all my ways.

Before a word is on my tongue you know it completely, O LORD....

Search me, O God, and know my heart; test me and know my anxious thoughts.

See if there is any offensive way in me, and lead me in the way everlasting.

CHARACTER CHECK
What key habits do I need to be more spiritually effective?

_____

_____

_____

_____

_____

IN BUSINESS TERMS

Historians continue to puzzle over one of the great mysteries of history: how to explain the sixteenth century. In 1560 two institutions dominated Europe, neither of which had existed twenty-five years earlier. The north was dominated by the Calvinist movement, the south by the Jesuit order.

In 1534 Ignatius Loyola gathered the nucleus of his new order and took the vows of poverty, chastity, and obedience. In 1536 John Calvin arrived in Geneva. Twenty-five years later, Europe had been changed. Nothing in the history of the world can compare with the rapid growth and effectiveness of these institutions.

How do you explain it? Both were, by 1560, large institutions, each involving thousands of ordinary people, most of them working alone. Many worked under great pressure and danger, yet there were practically no defections. Very few bad apples. What was the secret?

Now we understand it. Both Calvin and Loyola taught a similar spiritual discipline: that whenever one does anything in a key activity (they were usually spiritual activities, but not entirely), one writes it down, and then one keeps track of what happens. This feedback, whether it's a Calvinist examination of conscience or the Jesuit spiritual exercise, is the way you quickly find out what you're good at. And you find out what your bad habits are that inhibit full yield.

–Peter Drucker

SOMETHING TO THINK ABOUT

It is when we face ourselves and face Christ, that we are lost in wonder, love, and praise. We need to rediscover the almost lost discipline of self-examination; and then a reawakened sense of sin will beget a reawakened sense of wonder.

—

Andrew Murray

BETTER WITH AGE

THE BIBLE PLACES A PREMIUM ON OLD AGE. GRAY HAIR REFLECTS THE SPLENDOR OF A PERSON WHOM THE YEARS HAVE SEASONED. IN ANCIENT ISRAEL, OLDER PEOPLE DIDN'T RETIRE, THEY MOVED INTO LEADERSHIP ROLES. THE ELDERS WERE THE LEADERS OF VILLAGES AND TOWNS.

PROVERBS 1:8–9; 20:29; 23:22–25; 31:23

Listen, my son, to your father's instruction and do not forsake your mother's teaching. They will be a garland to grace your head and a chain to adorn your neck. . . .

The glory of young men is their strength, gray hair the splendor of the old. . . .

Listen to your father, who gave you life, and do not despise your mother when she is old. Buy the truth and do not sell it; get wisdom, discipline and understanding. The father of a righteous son has great joy; he who has a wise son delights in him. May your father and mother be glad; may she who gave you birth rejoice! . . .

Her husband is respected at the city gate, where he takes his seat among the elders of the land.

CHARACTER CHECK
Do I have a growing edge?

_____

_____

_____

_____

_____

IN BUSINESS TERMS

The youth culture says you're going to peak in your thirties: you're going to find out whether you're a major league player, a AAA player, a AA player, an A player, or whether you have been cut. Not knowing where you measure up in terms of the field is an uncertainty.

At the Indy 500, it doesn't do any good to blow up your engine in the qualifying laps, because if you're not running for the main event, you can't compete, let alone place. Yet many people suffer the delusion that the first half of life is the main event. They will sacrifice things that are irreplaceable in the effort to peak too soon. The family becomes the sacrificed commodity. Their faith becomes the compromised value.

I am convinced more all the time that life begins at fifty for our generation. So business leaders are asking, "How do you prepare to be in the race when the race really does begin?"

–Bob Shank

TRUTHTELLING VALUE

AT WORK, IT'S NOT ALWAYS WHAT WE SAY BUT WHAT WE DON'T SAY. TO BE FULLY TRUTHFUL SOMETIMES REQUIRES US TO ADMIT TO OTHERS OUR FEELINGS, WHICH MIGHT NOT SEEM ACCEPTABLE. PROVERBS RAISES UP THE VALUE OF TRUTHFULNESS, WHICH, IF COMMUNICATED PROPERLY, DEEPENS OUR RELATIONSHIPS, ESPECIALLY WITH OUR CLOSEST COLLEAGUES.

PROVERBS 10:18, 19; 12:19, 22; 16:13; 21:6, 28

He who conceals his hatred has lying lips, ...

but he who holds his tongue is wise. ...

Truthful lips endure forever,

but a lying tongue lasts only a moment. ...

The LORD detests lying lips,

but he delights in men who are truthful. ...

Kings take pleasure in honest lips;

they value a man who speaks the truth. ...

A fortune made by a lying tongue

is a fleeting vapor and a deadly snare. ...

A false witness will perish,

and whoever listens to him will be destroyed forever.

CHARACTER CHECK
Ask the Lord to help you be more open with others.

_____

_____

_____

_____

_____

IN BUSINESS TERMS

I first learned about the value of honesty in prison.

Not when I was in prison, but when in high school I visited a prison with my sociology class. Everyone, especially the guys, was acting totally cool, as if we'd been to lots of prisons, and prisoners didn't scare us, and we could handle ourselves. You know, smart remarks, jokes, all the guy baloney.

We were finally escorted into a room with three prisoners with whom we were going to talk. We all took our chairs in a circle and sat and stared at each other, everyone looking as cool as ever.

After introducing the men, the teacher asked if we had any questions. There was a long silence.

Margie, a tall, thin girl who appeared as in control as the rest of us, said, "I don't know about anyone else, but I'm kind of scared."

Everyone laughed–not at her, but with her: we were all feeling the same thing. And all of us, like Margie, had been putting on an act. Now, because of her honesty, we didn't have to.

With that, a genuine conversation with our hosts began.

–Mark Galli

INTOXICATED WITH LOVE

THE SPORTS CLICHÉ IS TRUE: THE BEST DEFENSE IS OFTEN A GOOD OFFENSE. AFTER URGING YOUNG MEN TO TAKE PRECAUTIONS TO AVOID SEXUAL TEMPTATION, PROVERBS ENCOURAGES THEM TO INTOXICATE THEMSELVES WITH THE LOVE OF THEIR WIVES. A STRONG SEXUAL RELATIONSHIP WITH ONE'S SPOUSE, WHICH BEGINS BY SPENDING TIME TOGETHER, MAKES AN EXTRAMARITAL AFFAIR LESS LIKELY.

PROVERBS 5:3–4, 15–21

For the lips of an adulteress drip honey, and her speech is smoother than oil; but in the end she is bitter as gall, sharp as a double-edged sword. . . .

Drink water from your own cistern, running water from your own well. Should your springs overflow in the streets, your streams of water in the public squares? Let them be yours alone, never to be shared with strangers.

May your fountain be blessed, and may you rejoice in the wife of your youth. A loving doe, a graceful deer–may her breasts satisfy you always, may you ever be captivated by her love.

Why be captivated, my son, by an adulteress? Why embrace the bosom of another man's wife? For a man's ways are in full view of the LORD, and he examines all his paths.

CHARACTER CHECK

How well do I communicate my expectations about sex with my spouse?

_____

_____

_____

_____

_____

IN BUSINESS TERMS

A husband and wife need to work at maintaining intellectual compatibility. My wife and I try to read together, go to movies and plays and museums together, and then go out together, just the two of us, and discuss what we've seen or read. That discussion is worth more to our relationship than the outing itself.

I know that with all the demands we face, including obligations to our children, finding the time to maintain this kind of relationship with a spouse isn't easy–far from it. But there is no more important human relationship in the world for us to maintain. It's worth the effort and time and money it takes.

Sexual temptation is all around us these days, and if we're honest with ourselves, we know we're often vulnerable. In spite of all we do to avoid tempting situations, there will be times when temptation will stare us right in the face. Our job is to prepare ourselves and keep our marriages strong *before* we find ourselves in those situations so that when the temptations come, we'll be able to maintain our integrity.

–Jay Kesler

SOMETHING TO THINK ABOUT

A good husband makes a good wife.

—

Anonymous

THE CASE FOR DILIGENCE

IN RECENT YEARS, A NEW TEMPTATION FOR SLOTH HAS EMERGED WITH THE INTERNET. PROFESSIONALS SPEND COMPANY TIME SURFING THE 'NET, EXPLORING WEB SITES AND CATCHING UP ON THE LATEST BASEBALL SCORES. PROVERBS 6 OFFERS AN "ANT DOCUMENTARY" TO MAKE A CASE FOR DILIGENCE. SLUGGARDS MAY SEEM TO HAVE IT EASY, BUT THEIR LIFESTYLE IS REALLY A KIND OF POVERTY.

PROVERBS 6:6–11

Go to the ant, you sluggard;

consider its ways and be wise!

It has no commander,

no overseer or ruler,

yet it stores its provisions in summer

and gathers its food at harvest.

How long will you lie there, you sluggard?

When will you get up from your sleep?

A little sleep, a little slumber, a little folding of the hands to rest–and

poverty will come on you like a bandit and scarcity like an armed man.

CHARACTER CHECK
How can I cut down on my busyness and yet be more fruitful?

IN BUSINESS TERMS

For a long time, I didn't understand the spiritual significance of sloth. I thought it was simply a matter of developing better work habits, becoming more motivated, or working harder or smarter.

A billion-dollar cottage industry–the motivational market–has emerged precisely because we no longer understand the true significance of sloth and hence don't know how to respond to it. We go from motivational speaker to seminar to book to tape, as if we were basketballs with slow leaks trying to find someone or something to pump us up, to counteract our tendency to deflate.

The Bible doesn't call us to be more motivated or more productive workers. The relevant image in Scripture is fruitfulness. Not busyness. Not even productivity.

A godly person, the Bible says, is like a tree planted by rivers of living waters. Trees are not frenzied or frantic. They do not attend seminars on "releasing the redwood within them." They do not consume vast amounts of caffeine to keep up their adrenaline. Trees are unhurried. They are full of activity, though most of it is unseen. Mostly, a tree knows from where its nourishment comes. It is deeply rooted. It is not easily distracted. A tree has learned to abide.

Abiding in Christ is the great antithesis to sloth. Abiding is effort–filled but is the place of nourishment and renewal.

–John Ortberg

TRUTH IN LOVE

"ALWAYS LEAVE A FEW THINGS UNSAID AT THE END OF THE DAY"—THAT'S GOOD ADVICE FOR BUSINESS OR FOR MARRIAGE. EVEN MORE DIFFICULT, THOUGH, IS WHEN YOU DECIDE TO CONFRONT SOMEBODY WITH A HARD WORD. SPEAKING TRUTHFULLY MAY REQUIRE A WORD OF CAUTION OR AN HONEST INSIGHT.

PROVERBS 10:19–20; 15:23; 18:6, 13; 25:12

When words are many, sin is not absent, but he who holds his tongue is wise. The tongue of the righteous is choice silver, but the heart of the wicked is of little value....

A man finds joy in giving an apt reply—and how good is a timely word!...

A fool's lips bring him strife, and his mouth invites a beating....

He who answers before listening—that is his folly and his shame....

Like an earring of gold or an ornament of fine gold is a wise man's rebuke to a listening ear.

CHARACTER CHECK
When I experience conflict with others do I tend to overspiritualize it?

_____

_____

_____

_____

_____

IN BUSINESS TERMS

So often prayer is used to say, "I don't think you're under-standing what I'm saying, and surely it must be because the Lord isn't making it clear to you. So let's stop and call upon him, so you can understand how right I am."

The trouble with using prayer in the middle of a board meeting at church is that it is often suggested just as the discussion is getting honest. People are finally saying what they've been thinking all night ("You know, you really did lie to me, Jack"), and some nervous soul sees the Spirit slipping away and quickly wants to have a word of prayer. What people really mean is, "I'm uncomfortable with how heavy this discussion is getting, and I want to retreat, so everybody bow your head." And it's very hard at that point to say, "No, let's not." The key moment is lost as the one side co-opts Jesus.

What we need to do in conflict is to talk to each other. God is quite capable of listening to our debate; we don't need to pause and say, "God, are you here?" He is also quite capable of informing our hearing and speaking.

–Lynn Buzzard

_____

_____

_____

_____

_____

MANAGING YOUR ANGER

"EMAIL REGRET" OCCURS WHEN YOU CLICK "SEND" BUT WISH YOU HADN'T. IN AN ANGRY IMPULSE YOU FIRE OFF A HOT EMAIL TO YOUR BOSS OR COLLEAGUE. NOW YOU CAN'T UNSEND YOUR MESSAGE. PROVERBS PROVIDES STRATEGIES FOR CONTROLLING YOUR TEMPER, INCLUDING REMEMBERING BEFOREHAND THE CONSEQUENCES OF AN ANGRY RESPONSE.

PROVERBS 15:1; 29:8, 11, 22; 30:33

A gentle answer turns away wrath, but a harsh word stirs up anger....

Mockers stir up a city, but wise men turn away anger....

A fool gives full vent to his anger, but a wise man keeps himself under control.

An angry man stirs up dissension, and a hot-tempered one commits many sins.

For as churning the milk produces butter, and as twisting the nose produces blood, so stirring up anger produces strife.

CHARACTER CHECK
How would my colleagues or spouse say I handle my anger?

_____

_____

_____

_____

_____

IN BUSINESS TERMS

Lots of people have the power to hurt or frustrate me. Only one has the power to make me angry. Me. If it's true that no one else can make me angry, it's even more true that no one else can make me respond aggressively or inappropriately when I feel anger. It often seems that way because my response to feeling anger has become so routine that it seems "automatic." It feels as if the person or event triggered my anger and caused my response.

The truth is, my response is learned behavior. I learned it long ago, from people I grew up around, learned it so informally that I was not aware I was learning anything.

Tommy Bolt has been described as the angriest golfer in the history of a game that has stimulated the secretion of more bile than any other human activity outside war and denominational meetings. One (possibly apocryphal) story recalls a time he was giving a group lesson on how to hit a ball out of a sand trap. He called his eleven-year-old son over.

"Show the people what you've learned from your father to do when your shot lands in the sand," he said. The boy picked up a wedge and threw it as high and as far as he could.

The good news is that what can be learned can be unlearned. It is possible for me to manage my anger in a God-honoring way: to "be angry and sin not." Anger is an inescapable fact of life. But the experience of anger is different from the expression of anger.

–John Ortberg

FRIENDS TO DIE FOR

REBUKE FROM A FRIEND IS ACTUALLY A FORM OF LOVE. THOUGH PAINFUL AT THE MOMENT, REBUKE IS PROFITABLE IN THE LONG RUN. WHEN REBUKE COMES FROM A FRIEND, YOU CAN TRUST THE SOURCE. YOU KNOW THE PERSON HAS YOUR BEST INTERESTS IN MIND. ACCEPTING REBUKE IS ONE THING, GIVING REBUKE ANOTHER. BOTH ARE NEEDED TO MAKE FRIENDSHIP THRIVE.

PROVERBS 15:21–22, 31–33, 27:5–6, 9, 17

Folly delights a man who lacks judgment, but a man of understanding keeps a straight course. Plans fail for lack of counsel, but with many advisers they succeed....

He who listens to a life-giving rebuke will be at home among the wise. He who ignores discipline despises himself, but whoever heeds correction gains understanding. The fear of the LORD teaches a man wisdom, and humility comes before honor....

Better is open rebuke than hidden love. Wounds from a friend can be trusted, but an enemy multiplies kisses....

Perfume and incense bring joy to the heart, and the pleasantness of one's friend springs from his earnest counsel....

As iron sharpens iron, so one man sharpens another.

CHARACTER CHECK
Do I have a friend who needs me to tell him or her the truth?

_____

_____

_____

_____

_____

IN BUSINESS TERMS

In ordinary life the people we like, our friends, are the people we find most difficult to rebuke. Yet, precisely with a friend, difficult advice goes deepest. Most of us don't pay much attention to the critique of people we know don't like us. However, we listen to our friends because we know they have our best interests in mind. But even deeper, we listen to our friends–even though doing so may hurt–because they know us at our best, they love us at our best, and they know when we are violating our own best self. No one but a friend knows when we are really hurting and when we need compassion, or when we are whining and need someone to kick us off the dead self-centeredness of self-pity. It's a difficult choice to live in loyal bond with friends whom the Word, Spirit, and conscience force us to discipline. That is the sign of being a leader.
It doesn't feel nice. But it requires the love of a leader.

    –Dave Hansen

SOMETHING TO THINK ABOUT

The truth does not change according to our ability to stomach it.

—

Flannery O'Connor

PART OF THE GREAT PLAN

AT THE END OF THE DAY, NEAR THE END OF A LIFE, WHAT DOES A PERSON'S WORK ADD UP TO? WHAT DOES IT ALL MEAN? THE WRITER OF ECCLESIASTES POSED THE SAME QUESTION. THE ANSWER IS THAT GOD DOESN'T ALWAYS SHOW US THE ANSWER IN THIS LIFE. HE ASKS US TO FIND SATISFACTION IN OUR WORK BECAUSE WE ARE CONFIDENT THAT IT IS GOD'S GIFT.

ECCLESIASTES 3:9–15

What does the worker gain from his toil? I have seen the burden God has laid on men. He has made everything beautiful in its time. He has also set eternity in the hearts of men; yet they cannot fathom what God has done from beginning to end. I know that there is nothing better for men than to be happy and do good while they live. That everyone may eat and drink, and find satisfaction in all his toil–this is the gift of God. I know that everything God does will endure forever; nothing can be added to it and nothing taken from it. God does it so that men will revere him.

Whatever is has already been, and what will be has been before; and God will call the past to account.

CHARACTER CHECK
What could I do this week to let God transform some aspect of my job?

_____

_____

_____

_____

_____

IN BUSINESS TERMS

Contentment in your work comes from standing constantly and consciously in the presence of God so that he can transform any task into something meaningful.

I read of a checker at a Safeway supermarket in Oakland, California, some years back. Her job wasn't ideal, but she had figured out ways to transform that job. She'd tap out a rhythm you could almost tap-dance to as she rang up items on the cash register. She'd offer recipes to customers. She had a jar of cookies at her side to hand out to kids. And to beat the monotony of bagging the groceries, she played a game with herself, figuring out the cleverest way to fit the most items into the bag. She made packing bags an art.

People often see vocational contentment as a happy match between what you have to do and what you enjoy doing. But there's no such permanent match. When you define contentment as an ideal match, which I did for years, you're subject to the fact that it's like passion: it often doesn't last long.

But when you define contentment as the ability to let God transform your job, then you'll find contentment.

–Richard Nelson Bolles

SOMETHING TO THINK ABOUT

There are three kinds of people: those who have sought God and found him, and these are reasonable and happy; those who seek God and have not yet found him, and these are reasonable and unhappy; and those who neither seek God nor find him, and these are unreasonable and unhappy.

—

Blaise Pascal

ONE AMONG FRIENDS

IN BUSINESS, GREAT ACHIEVEMENTS ARE GENERALLY THE RESULT OF EFFECTIVE
TEAMS. THE PERSON WHO TRIES TO STAND ALONE WILL QUICKLY LOSE STRENGTH AND
ENTHUSIASM. EVEN JESUS, THOUGH HE WAS GOD AND COULD HAVE DONE EVERY-
THING BY HIMSELF, CHOSE TO GATHER A GROUP OF KEY FOLLOWERS TO HELP HIM
CARRY OUT HIS EARTHLY MINISTRY AND TO KEEP HIM COMPANY ALONG THE WAY.

ECCLESIASTES 4:7–12

Again I saw something meaningless under the sun:

*There was a man all alone; he had neither son nor brother. There was
no end to his toil, yet his eyes were not content with his wealth. "For
whom am I toiling," he asked, "and why am I depriving myself of enjoy-
ment?" This too is meaningless—a miserable business!*

*Two are better than one, because they have a good return for their
work:*

*If one falls down, his friend can help him up. But pity the man who
falls and has no one to help him up! Also, if two lie down together, they
will keep warm. But how can one keep warm alone? Though one may
be overpowered, two can defend themselves. A cord of three strands is
not quickly broken.*

CHARACTER CHECK

What is the next step I should take to move that friendship forward?

_____

_____

_____

_____

_____

IN BUSINESS TERMS

I depend on the leadership team at our church. An important part of our meetings is the sharing of our needs. I feel I must lead the way, since my vulnerability will give permission to others to be honest. Often, I'll open our sharing with a confession of need or a problem I'm facing. After someone has shared, we pray for him or her.

We maximize the joys together, too, and that's important to keep one's enthusiasm alive. The test of friendship is that you can share the great things that have happened as well as the frustrating ones. Lots of people are happy to share your failures with you, but it takes a great friend to listen to victories and say, "Isn't it wonderful? Let's rejoice together."

I couldn't handle the demands I have on me if it weren't for a healing center of fellowship in which I can be absolutely open and honest, be loved and challenged, and then be prayed for as a brother.

–Lloyd John Ogilvie

SOMETHING TO THINK ABOUT

We love those who know the worst of us and don't turn their faces away.

—

Walker Percy

ALTERED REALITY

TRAVELING ABROAD OFTEN PUTS US FACE TO FACE WITH RAW HUMAN NEED. MOST PEOPLE OF THE WORLD LIVE CHAINED TO POVERTY. ONCE CONFRONTED WITH ABJECT POVERTY, MOST PEOPLE CANNOT PUT OUT OF THEIR MIND THE STENCH, THE FLIES, THE CRIES OF HUNGRY INFANTS. THEIR REALITY HAS BEEN PERMANENTLY ALTERED. SO IT IS WHEN WE ENCOUNTER THE LIVING GOD.

ISAIAH 6:1–5

In the year that King Uzziah died, I saw the Lord seated on a throne, high and exalted, and the train of his robe filled the temple. Above him were seraphs, each with six wings: With two wings they covered their faces, with two they covered their feet, and with two they were flying. And they were calling to one another:

"Holy, holy, holy is the LORD Almighty;

the whole earth is full of his glory."

At the sound of their voices the doorposts and thresholds shook and the temple was filled with smoke.

"Woe to me!" I cried. "I am ruined! For I am a man of unclean lips, and I live among a people of unclean lips, and my eyes have seen the King, the LORD Almighty."

CHARACTER CHECK
When was the last time I sensed the presence of God?

_____

_____

_____

_____

_____

IN BUSINESS TERMS

Peak Moments. That's the phrase Outside magazine (October 1998) used to describe an "outsized moment, some breakthrough, I-just-didn't-realize instant when your relationship with the natural world pivots, expands, and is forever transformed."

Outside published six one-page accounts of people who came face to face with the awesomeness or terribleness of nature. For example, one firefighter, David Guterson, describes how he was almost burned alive by a raging forest fire. "Chased by the fire, I ran like a madman, and then splashed into a low creek, where I drank, doused my head, and vomited. A revelatory moment, of sorts. I had been fighting fire all that summer, but I hadn't yet reckoned with its elemental power. Now I understood its deification of the terrible god of annihilation."

That reckoning changed Guterson forever. He wrote, "It was as though I had eaten from the Tree of Knowledge. My corporeality was clarified. I was no different from a rump roast, a ham. I was 19, and made of tender flesh." In an instant, Guterson saw the world differently. Reality shifted, and he was never the same.

The Old Testament prophet Isaiah also had a peak moment, when he saw the Lord "seated on a throne, high and exalted, and the train of his robe filled the temple . . . 'Woe to me!' I cried. 'I am ruined! For I am a man of unclean lips.'" Isaiah had entered into the terrible and awesome presence of holy God.

I am asking God to give me every once in a while a peak moment, a glimpse into the mystery and presence of God. I want the life-altering, reality-defining experience of knowing God.

–David L. Goetz

NOT OFF THE HOOK

GOD OFTEN CALLS HIS PEOPLE TO DIFFICULT TASKS. ISAIAH'S TOUGH JOB ASSIGNMENT WAS SPEAKING TO PEOPLE WHO WOULD REFUSE TO LISTEN. GOD DOESN'T LET US OFF THE HOOK BY OFFERING US A LIFE OF EASE. HE KNOWS THAT WHEN WE ARE STRETCHED AND CHALLENGED, WE GROW.

ISAIAH 6:8–13

Then I heard the voice of the Lord saying, "Whom shall I send? And who will go for us?"

And I said, "Here am I. Send me!"

He said, "Go and tell this people: 'Be ever hearing, but never understanding; be ever seeing, but never perceiving.'

"Make the heart of this people callused; make their ears dull and close their eyes. Otherwise they might see with their eyes, hear with their ears, understand with their hearts, and turn and be healed."

Then I said, "For how long, O Lord?" And he answered:

"Until the cities lie ruined and without inhabitant, until the houses are left deserted and the fields ruined and ravaged, until the LORD has sent everyone far away and the land is utterly forsaken. And though a tenth remains in the land, it will again be laid waste. But as the terebinth and oak leave stumps when they are cut down, so the holy seed will be the stump in the land."

CHARACTER CHECK

What challenging work is Jesus calling me to this week?

_____

_____

_____

_____

_____

IN BUSINESS TERMS

In the church sometimes we'll call up somebody in mid-August and say, "Sorry we're late, but we wonder if you would like to teach the eighth grade Sunday school class starting right after Labor Day? It doesn't take much preparation. It's not a lot of hard work. You can do it. We know you can."

That's no way to get anybody to reach his or her potential. It's wrong to offer people easy work. Few things in life are more insulting than to be offered an easy job.

Many years ago my wife and I attended a church that was having some special problems with a high school class. These kids were tough to handle. So they asked a capable, experienced woman in the church to help.

"Mary," they said, "we'd like you to take this class. They're unmanageable, and we don't know what can be done with them."

They challenged her in a wonderful way.

–Max De Pree

SOMETHING TO THINK ABOUT

The job of a football coach is to make men do what they don't want to do, in order to achieve what they've always wanted to be.

—

Tom Landry

UNLIKELY BESTSELLER

MANY BUSINESS AND PROFESSIONAL PEOPLE ARE DRAWN TO BOOKS AND SEMINARS PROMISING THE SECRETS OF SUCCESS, WEALTH, AND HAPPINESS. NOBODY EVER WROTE A BESTSELLER TITLED *REPENT!* BUT THAT'S EXACTLY WHAT GOD CALLS US TO DO WHEN WE FOLLOW HIM. JESUS OFFERS MORE THAN HAPPINESS, AS IT IS DEFINED BY THE CULTURE AROUND US.

ISAIAH 48:1–2, 9–11

"Listen to this, O house of Jacob, you who are called by the name of Israel and come from the line of Judah, you who take oaths in the name of the LORD and invoke the God of Israel–but not in truth or righteousness–you who call yourselves citizens of the holy city and rely on the God of Israel . . .

"For my own name's sake I delay my wrath; for the sake of my praise I hold it back from you, so as not to cut you off.

"See, I have refined you, though not as silver; I have tested you in the furnace of affliction. For my own sake, for my own sake, I do this. How can I let myself be defamed? I will not yield my glory to another."

CHARACTER CHECK
Where am I resisting God in my life?

_____

_____

_____

_____

_____

IN BUSINESS TERMS

We exist for God. God, in his great mercy, has promised that blessedness will accompany discipleship, but it's got to be God first.

Without that, to say that Christianity is the secret of happiness is dangerous. Often evangelists who preach that way leave the wrong impression and confirm the egocentricity of folk, who then try Christianity as a formula for happiness. God is merciful, and sometimes there is a real conversion and real regeneration. But even so, that kind of teaching is likely to produce substandard saints.

You don't actually help the butterfly emerge from its chrysalis by cutting the chrysalis. If the butterfly doesn't struggle from inside to get out, it comes out as a butterfly that isn't strong enough to fly. People who get into the Christian life without ever being challenged to repent of their egocentricity are, at best, likely to remain stunted Christians.

The struggle to change at this point is necessary for health and growth.

–J. I. Packer

SOMETHING TO THINK ABOUT

The smallest package I ever saw was a man wrapped up wholly in himself.

—

Billy Graham

SPIRITUAL PASSION

EVEN THE GOOD THINGS IN LIFE CAN BECOME BAD. THE OLD TESTAMENT PROPHET JEREMIAH WARNED AGAINST MAKING SUCH THINGS AS WISDOM, STRENGTH, OR WEALTH THE DRIVING PASSIONS OF OUR LIFE. GOD OFFERS SOMETHING BETTER— THE BEST—HIMSELF.

JEREMIAH 9:23–24; 1 CORINTHIANS 1:26–27

This is what the LORD says:

"Let not the wise man boast of his wisdom or the strong man boast of his strength or the rich man boast of his riches, but let him who boasts boast about this: that he understands and knows me, that I am the LORD, who exercises kindness, justice and righteousness on earth, for in these I delight," declares the LORD.

Brothers, think of what you were when you were called. Not many of you were wise by human standards; not many were influential; not many were of noble birth. But God chose the foolish things of the world to shame the wise; God chose the weak things of the world to shame the strong. . . . so that no one may boast before him.

CHARACTER CHECK
In what area of my life am I sacrificing the best for merely the good?

_____

_____

_____

_____

_____

IN BUSINESS TERMS

I commit myself to projects and plans, and then wonder how I can get them all done. This is true of the pastor, the teacher, the administrator. Indeed, it's true of our culture, which tells us, "Do as much as you can or you'll never make it."

In that sense, we are part of the world.

I've discovered I cannot fight the demons of busyness directly. I cannot continuously say "No" to this or "No" to that, unless there is something ten times more attractive to choose. Saying "No" to my lust, my greed, my needs, and the world's powers takes an enormous amount of energy.

The only hope is to find something so obviously real and attractive that I can devote all my energies to saying "Yes." In effect, I don't have time to pay any attention to the distractions.

–Henri Nouwen

SOMETHING TO THINK ABOUT

Let us think often that our only business in this life is to please God.

—

Brother Lawrence

COURAGE TO STAND

MANY OF US, STRUGGLE TO FIND AND TAKE OPPORTUNITIES TO SPEAK UP FOR JESUS CHRIST. BUT THERE ARE MANY WAYS TO SPEAK UP FOR CHRIST OTHER THAN SIMPLY TALKING. THE OLD TESTAMENT CHARACTER DANIEL, AS A YOUNG MAN, STOOD UP AGAINST THE ORDER OF A POWERFUL KING. GOD USED DANIEL'S COURAGE TO SHAPE A WORLD LEADER.

DANIEL 1:5, 8–10

The king assigned them [Daniel and his fellow countrymen from Judah] a daily amount of food and wine from the king's table. They were to be trained for three years, and after that they were to enter the king's service. . . .

But Daniel resolved not to defile himself with the royal food and wine, and he asked the chief official for permission not to defile himself this way. Now God had caused the official to show favor and sympathy to Daniel, but the official told Daniel, "I am afraid of my lord the king, who has assigned your food and drink. Why should he see you looking worse than the other young men your age? The king would then have my head because of you."

CHARACTER CHECK
How have I recently shown integrity at work?

_____

_____

_____

_____

_____

IN BUSINESS TERMS

In *Leading with Integrity,* Fred Smith, Sr., an executive with Genesco for many years, wrote, "I heard the Jewish writer Chaim Potok say a true leader is never absorbed into the stream in which he swims. . . . The integrity of a leader often is shown in the stand he takes for right against mistaken popular concepts."

For the business professional, not to be absorbed into the culture of his or her work may mean different things. For some, that may mean deciding not to take a promotion so their family doesn't have to move cross-country again. Their decision cuts across the grain of the mistaken notion that family always takes a back seat to career. For others, that may mean speaking out against a corporate culture that tacitly permits sexual harassment. Both decisions may have serious consequences.

I often wonder what would have happened if Daniel hadn't taken a stand. At the very least, the high-stakes drama of Daniel in the court of the Babylonian king would never have played out. Because Daniel was not absorbed in the stream of Babylonian culture, he allowed himself to be used of God in a mighty way.

–David L. Goetz

SOMETHING TO THINK ABOUT

Courage faces fear and thereby masters it. Cowardice represses fear and is thereby mastered by it.

—

Martin Luther King, Jr.

_____
_____
_____
_____
_____

SMALL POTATOES

THERE ARE TIMES WHEN OUR WORK AND EFFORTS CAN FEEL LIKE SMALL POTATOES, TRIV-
IAL AND INSIGNIFICANT, ESPECIALLY WHEN WE COMPARE OURSELVES TO SOMEONE MORE
SUCCESSFUL. PEOPLE IN HAGGAI'S DAY WERE PAINFULLY AWARE THAT THEIR TEMPLE
COULDN'T HOLD A CANDLE TO THE MAGNIFICENT EDIFICE BUILT BY SOLOMON. BUT GOD
WANTED THEM TO REALIZE THAT NO WORK IS SMALL WHEN HE, THE LORD, IS IN IT.

HAGGAI 2:3–7, 9

"Who of you is left who saw this house in its former glory? How does it look to you now? Does it not seem to you like nothing? But now be strong, O Zerubbabel," declares the LORD. "Be strong, O Joshua son of Jehozadak, the high priest. Be strong, all you people of the land," declares the LORD, "and work. For I am with you," declares the LORD Almighty. "This is what I covenanted with you when you came out of Egypt. And my Spirit remains among you. Do not fear."

This is what the LORD Almighty says: "In a little while I will once more shake the heavens and the earth, the sea and the dry land. I will shake all nations, and the desired of all nations will come, and I will fill this house with glory. . . . And in this place I will grant peace."

CHARACTER CHECK
In what area of my life do I feel small? How has God used that for his glory?

_____

_____

_____

_____

_____

IN BUSINESS TERMS

The Bible says we should not despise the day of small things. God's work is done "not by might nor by power but by my Spirit."

For instance, I'm praying for a person losing his well-paid position with IBM. His wife is in agony about all the changes, so we've been looking to God for answers. God impressed upon me that this woman had been hurt so many times that she no longer could believe in God's goodness. With that knowledge, I knew I should pray that she would see the goodness of God in order to remove the fear that stems from all her hurts.

We shouldn't see this kind of surrender as some heroic deed to become spiritual. Instead it should be a release to God. People who are discontented and angry at God about their day of small things miss the chance for God to do something in their lives.

Wherever we are–in our family, in our community, in our education, even in our culture–no matter how small or despised that place may be, that is where God can use us and bless us. We may not achieve the dreams of our youth, but we can be sure God will bring us into the dreams he has for us.

–Dallas Willard

_____

_____

_____

_____

_____

OVERCOMING SELF-DOUBT

A CORNER OFFICE WITH THE BIG WINDOWS WILL NEVER STOP SELF-DOUBTS. EVEN THE MOST OUTWARDLY CONFIDENT ACHIEVERS OFTEN STRUGGLE WITH SELF-ACCEPTANCE. CHRIST GIVES US INNER STRENGTH AND COMPLETE ACCEPTANCE, WHICH ARE THE BASIS FOR A HEALTHY SELF-WORTH.

MATTHEW 5:3-12

"Blessed are the poor in spirit, for theirs is the kingdom of heaven.

"Blessed are those who mourn, for they will be comforted.

"Blessed are the meek, for they will inherit the earth.

"Blessed are those who hunger and thirst for righteousness, for they will be filled.

"Blessed are the merciful, for they will be shown mercy.

"Blessed are the pure in heart, for they will see God.

"Blessed are the peacemakers, for they will be called sons of God.

"Blessed are those who are persecuted because of righteousness, for theirs is the kingdom of heaven.

"Blessed are you when people insult you, persecute you and falsely say all kinds of evil against you because of me. Rejoice and be glad, because great is your reward in heaven, for in the same way they persecuted the prophets who were before you."

CHARACTER CHECK

Do I see myself as God sees me—as a beloved child?

IN BUSINESS TERMS

For years I struggled with a low self-image. Mother married my father against her parents' will. My father was an itinerant worker. He'd ride railroad freight cars to the Midwest, where he worked as a harvest laborer. Then he would return to his home in St. Paul and live on his wages. He was a kind person, soft-spoken, gentle; but my mother soon discovered that he was completely irresponsible. He never did support the family. My mother's father set him up in business twice, but he never made it go.

When I was ten years old my parents divorced—in a little North Dakota town where nobody got divorced—and we moved into a flat where we shared a bathroom with twenty families. I can still hear the cockroaches crush in the door jamb when I closed the door.

I've been afraid of my father's traits all my life. To this day, I feel there is something in me that wants to run as far away from responsibility as I can get.

After I became a Christian, a pastor helped me see my arrogance; that there was no substance to it, and I was covering up all those awful fears I had about myself and my inadequacy. He showed me how to study the Scriptures.

The verse that helped me turn the corner was Paul's marvelous testimony that in his weakness Christ became strong. In an incredible passage, 1 Corinthians 15, Paul said, "Last of all [Christ] appeared to me also, as to one abnormally born. For I am the least of the apostles and do not even deserve to be called an apostle, because I persecuted the church of God. But by the grace of God I am what I am."

I grabbed that truth with both hands as my valid place of self-acceptance; by the grace of God, I am what I am.

–Richard C. Halverson

SOMETHING TO THINK ABOUT

God doesn't use us based on what we look like. He uses us based on the condition of our souls.

—

Judith Couchman

DOWNWARD MOBILITY

FEW OF US HANG OUT WITH PEOPLE WHO HAVE LESS THAN WE DO. MOST OF US DON'T SET OUT TO AVOID HURTING, BROKEN, POOR PEOPLE; IT'S JUST THAT IN OUR RELATIONSHIPS, GRAVITY TENDS TO PULL US UP INSTEAD OF DOWN. BUT JESUS SPENT AT LEAST AS MUCH TIME WITH THE HURTING AS HE DID WITH THE HEALTHY. JESUS SAW THESE PEOPLE AS NEEDY AND DESERVING OF GOD'S LOVE.

MARK 2:13–17

Once again Jesus went out beside the lake. A large crowd came to him, and he began to teach them. As he walked along, he saw Levi son of Alphaeus sitting at the tax collector's booth. "Follow me," Jesus told him, and Levi got up and followed him.

While Jesus was having dinner at Levi's house, many tax collectors and "sinners" were eating with him and his disciples, for there were many who followed him. When the teachers of the law who were Pharisees saw him eating with the "sinners" and tax collectors, they asked his disciples: "Why does he eat with tax collectors and 'sinners'?"

On hearing this, Jesus said to them, "It is not the healthy who need a doctor, but the sick. I have not come to call the righteous, but sinners."

CHARACTER CHECK
How can I find time to spend with people who aren't "like me"?

_____

_____

_____

_____

_____

IN BUSINESS TERMS

One positive tension that indicates spiritual health is the ability to walk in God's presence and enjoy him for ourselves, yet still feel the world's hurts.

Recently it struck me that I run around with pretty good people: they're friendly, creative, fun to be with, and for the most part well-educated. My friendships were causing me to miss seeing the world through the eyes of the broken, lonely, and downtrodden.

I decided I needed to do something to change my perspective, so I went to night court. In Nashville, all the arrests made in our county, as well as in the city itself, are brought in before a magistrate during night court. Fifty seats are available for spectators.

As I watched the parade of people, suddenly I realized, *Hey, we're not winning.* The kind of people I hang around with are not typical. I saw broken families, I saw drunkenness and poverty, I saw the victims of fighting and cutting, the rawest kind of life you can imagine. I discovered I was completely out of touch with the hurts of people.

Befriending pretty good people had caused me to ignore a world in pain.

–Danny Morris

SOMETHING TO THINK ABOUT

We don't like lepers and losers very well; we prefer climbers and comers. For Christians, the temptation to be conformed to this world is desperately sweet and strong. Yet, says the apostle Paul, we are children of God if we suffer with Christ.

—

Cornelius Plantinga, Jr.

_____

_____

_____

_____

_____

WONDERFULLY MADE

JESUS USED A SMALL-GROUP STRATEGY TO SHAPE A GENERATION OF LEADERS.
ACCORDING TO MARK 3, JESUS GATHERED HIS SMALL GROUP OF TWELVE DISCIPLES
"TO BE WITH HIM" AND THEN TO TRAIN THEM TO DO MINISTRY.

MARK 3:13–19

*Jesus went up on a mountainside and called to him those he want-
ed, and they came to him. He appointed twelve–designating them apostles–that they might be with him and that he might send them out to
preach and to have authority to drive out demons. These are the twelve
he appointed: Simon (to whom he gave the name Peter); James son of
Zebedee and his brother John (to them he gave the name Boanerges,
which means Sons of Thunder); Andrew, Philip, Bartholomew, Matthew,
Thomas, James son of Alphaeus, Thaddaeus, Simon the Zealot, and
Judas Iscariot, who betrayed him.*

CHARACTER CHECK
Is my sense of who I am larger than simply my role at work or at home?

IN BUSINESS TERMS

People are not hired, paid, or rewarded for being balanced, whole human beings in their work environment. They're rewarded for being highly specialized and for being on someone else's agenda–the large company's agenda, the law firm's agenda, the client's requirements. A lot of people lose touch with the "me" underneath all the performing.

Management expert Peter Drucker once told me that's why people go to pubs. There, they discover what he calls the "third person." The first person is the work person–the role you are at work. The second person is the role you are when you walk in your home. The third person is who you are when not confined by those other two roles. Perhaps the church equivalent of a pub is a small group. There, in a group setting, you're able to be that person God designed you to be. You're not circumscribed by your roles as sales vice-president or parent.

–Bob Buford

_____

_____

_____

_____

_____

BIGGER THAN WE IMAGINE

EVEN THE MOST EXPERIENCED GARDENER CAN'T QUITE EXPLAIN HOW A HANDFUL OF TINY PELLETS TURNS INTO, SAY, A PLANT LADEN WITH TOMATOES. SO JESUS' COMPARISON OF THE KINGDOM OF GOD TO SEEDS IS A COMPELLING IMAGE. THOUGH OUR ATTEMPTS TO DO GOD'S WORK RESEMBLE SEEDS—SMALL AND INSIGNIFICANT—THEY WILL RESULT IN SOMETHING LARGER THAN WE CAN IMAGINE.

MARK 4:26–32

He also said, "This is what the kingdom of God is like. A man scatters seed on the ground. Night and day, whether he sleeps or gets up, the seed sprouts and grows, though he does not know how. All by itself the soil produces grain–first the stalk, then the head, then the full kernel in the head. As soon as the grain is ripe, he puts the sickle to it, because the harvest has come."

Again he said, "What shall we say the kingdom of God is like, or what parable shall we use to describe it? It is like a mustard seed, which is the smallest seed you plant in the ground. Yet when planted, it grows and becomes the largest of all garden plants, with such big branches that the birds of the air can perch in its shade."

CHARACTER CHECK
Where am I planting spiritual seeds?

_____

_____

_____

_____

_____

IN BUSINESS TERMS

On September 6, 1622, the Spanish galleon *Atocha,* bristling with bronze cannon and laden with gold and silver, served as the rear guard of a twenty-eight-vessel flotilla in the Gulf of Mexico. A hurricane struck, and the *Atocha* sank near the Marquesas Keys off the Florida coast, where she remained for 365 years.

In the 1980s a treasure hunter and a college professor who had pored over Spanish documents of the voyage found the *Atocha.* Among those who examined the ship's contents was an archaeologist, and in the sand that had served as its ballast he found something of special interest: seeds. To keep them from drying out he put the seeds in cups of fresh water. Nine days later as he checked the water level in the cups, he made his own surprising discovery: "Suddenly, I saw leaves sticking up," he says. To his astonishment four of the seeds had sprouted.

As this account shows, the seeds of this natural world are miracles endued by God with the power of life. Can the seeds of the spiritual world be any less powerful?

–Craig Brian Larson

TOTAL TRUST

No employee can thrive in a corporate culture devoid of trust. Trust is one of the basic bonds of relationships. Trust is also one of the basic bonds of our relationship with God. The Bible records that the disciples of Jesus struggled with trusting him. While the disciples had seen Jesus do miracles, they weren't prepared to trust Christ for just everything.

MARK 8:14–21

The disciples had forgotten to bring bread, except for one loaf they had with them in the boat. "Be careful," Jesus warned them. "Watch out for the yeast of the Pharisees and that of Herod."

They discussed this with one another and said, "It is because we have no bread."

Aware of their discussion, Jesus asked them: "Why are you talking about having no bread? Do you still not see or understand? Are your hearts hardened? Do you have eyes but fail to see, and ears but fail to hear? And don't you remember? When I broke the five loaves for the five thousand, how many basketfuls of pieces did you pick up?"

"Twelve," they replied.

"And when I broke the seven loaves for the four thousand, how many basketfuls of pieces did you pick up?" They answered, "Seven."

He said to them, "Do you still not understand?"

CHARACTER CHECK
In what area of my life do I need to trust God to provide?

_____

_____

_____

_____

_____

IN BUSINESS TERMS

There's little difference in ethical behavior between the churched and the unchurched. There's as much pilferage and dishonesty among the churched as the unchurched. I'm afraid that applies pretty much across the board: religion, per se, is not really life changing. People cite it as important, for instance, in overcoming depression—but it doesn't have primacy in determining behavior.

Recently, for the Christian Broadcasting Network, we asked a series of questions on whether people rely more on human reason or on an outside power, such as God, for moral guidance and for planning for their future. More opted for human reason than for God, although less so among evangelicals. That shows that whatever people say about their beliefs, when they get right down to it, they are not totally prepared to trust God.

–George H. Gallup, Jr.

SOMETHING TO THINK ABOUT

Faith begins where man's power ends.

—

George Miller

LEADING BY SERVING

SERVING OTHERS IN BUSINESS SOUNDS GOOD, BUT FEW ACHIEVE IT. THE TEMPTA-
TION IN MANAGING PEOPLE IS TO USE PEOPLE RATHER THAN DEVELOP THEM. WHEN
TWO DISCIPLES OF JESUS REQUESTED A PLACE OF PROMINENCE IN JESUS' KINGDOM,
JESUS INSTRUCTED THE DISCIPLES ON THE TRUE MEANING OF LEADERSHIP—NOT
"LORD-LEADERSHIP," BUT SERVANT LEADERSHIP.

MARK 10:35–37, 42–45

*Then James and John, the sons of Zebedee, came to him. "Teacher,"
they said, "we want you to do for us whatever we ask."*

*They replied, "Let one of us sit at your right and the other at your
left in your glory...."*

*Jesus called them together and said, "You know that those who are
regarded as rulers of the Gentiles lord it over them, and their high officials exercise authority over them. Not so with you. Instead, whoever
wants to become great among you must be your servant, and whoever
wants to be first must be slave of all.*

*For even the Son of Man did not come to be served, but to serve,
and to give his life as a ransom for many."*

CHARACTER CHECK
How does my ego prevent me from servant leadership at work or at home?

_____

_____

_____

_____

_____

IN BUSINESS TERMS

Often we announce a destination: "Here's a vision; here's what I want to do." Then we use a delegating leadership style and don't roll up our sleeves and get in there.

That's what managing the journey is. Sure, it's coming up with the vision and the direction, but then the vision must be implemented: coaching, supporting, giving directions, praising progress, and redirecting.

Jesus did this well. I told consultants Tom Peters and Robert Waterman, who wrote *In Search of Excellence,* "You didn't invent management by wandering around. Jesus did." He wandered from one little town to another, and people would say, "How do you become first?" Jesus said, "By being last."

People would ask him, "How do you lead?" "By following."

How many people do you know who go to their boss's house for dinner and the boss says, "Take off your shoes and socks and let me wash your feet"?

Managing the journey of change is servant leadership. We must get our egos out of the way and praise, redirect, reprimand–anything it takes to help people win.

–Ken Blanchard

SOMETHING TO THINK ABOUT

God did not write solo parts for very many of us. He expects us to be participants in the great symphony of life.

—

Donald Tippett

THE DONOR LIST

EVEN IN THE CHURCH, THE PEOPLE WITH MONEY TO GIVE ARE OFTEN AWARDED POWER AND PRIVILEGE. BUT IN THE NEW TESTAMENT, THE BIG-TIME GIVER WAS A WOMAN WHO CONTRIBUTED LESS THAN A NICKEL. JESUS AWARDED HER THE TROPHY FOR GIVING.

MARK 12:41–44; 2 CORINTHIANS 9:6–7

Jesus sat down opposite the place where the offerings were put and watched the crowd putting their money into the temple treasury. Many rich people threw in large amounts. But a poor widow came and put in two very small copper coins, worth only a fraction of a penny.

Calling his disciples to him, Jesus said, "I tell you the truth, this poor widow has put more into the treasury than all the others. They all gave out of their wealth, but she, out of her poverty, put in everything–all she had to live on."

Remember this: Whoever sows sparingly will also reap sparingly, and whoever sows generously will also reap generously. Each man should give what he has decided in his heart to give, not reluctantly or under compulsion, for God loves a cheerful giver.

CHARACTER CHECK
How sacrificial is my giving to the church?

_____

_____

_____

_____

_____

IN BUSINESS TERMS

I believe God honors many poor people who don't give a tenth, because what they do give is a sacrificial amount in relationship to what they earn. Similarly, for many wealthy people, giving a tenth is a way of robbing God. Their tithe becomes a tip.

I'm impressed by the formula of John Wesley, who, when he made thirty pounds, lived on twenty-eight pounds and gave away two. Then he made sixty pounds, but he knew he could live on twenty-eight pounds, so he gave away thirty-two. The next year, his income rose to ninety pounds, but he still lived on twenty-eight pounds and gave away the rest.

From a biblical perspective, the amount or percentage someone gives is not the real issue. What's critical is the giver's attitude and level of sacrifice.

–Haddon Robinson

SOMETHING TO THINK ABOUT

Our faith becomes practical when it is expressed in two books: the date book and the check book.

—

Elton Trueblood

TIME FOR THE IMPORTANT

SOMEONE ONCE SAID THAT TOO OFTEN WE RUN ON FUMES RATHER THAN OUT OF A FULL TANK. WHAT'S TRULY MOST IMPORTANT (REFRESHING AND RENEWING OUR SPIRITS) ALWAYS TAKES A BACK SEAT TO THE URGENT (THE PEOPLE AND PROJECTS NEEDING ATTENTION). EVEN WITH THE TREMENDOUS DEMANDS ON HIM, HOWEVER, JESUS WITHDREW TO SEEK HIS FATHER IN PRAYER.

LUKE 5:12–16

While Jesus was in one of the towns, a man came along who was covered with leprosy. When he saw Jesus, he fell with his face to the ground and begged him, "Lord, if you are willing, you can make me clean."

Jesus reached out his hand and touched the man. "I am willing," he said. "Be clean!" And immediately the leprosy left him.

Then Jesus ordered him, "Don't tell anyone, but go, show yourself to the priest and offer the sacrifices that Moses commanded for your cleansing, as a testimony to them."

Yet the news about him spread all the more, so that crowds of people came to hear him and to be healed of their sicknesses. But Jesus often withdrew to lonely places and prayed.

CHARACTER CHECK
What part of my day is best for creating space for solitude?

_____

_____

_____

_____

_____

IN BUSINESS TERMS

Christian solitude is often misunderstood. Moderns tend to think of it as "getting away from it all." In the Chicago area where I live, those who can afford it buy cabins on a lake in Wisconsin. In addition to commuting an hour or more each day for work, many then commute several hours north on weekends to find rest from the craziness of suburban living. A friend recently sold his townhouse in Wisconsin, though, because the weekend commute defeated the purpose of owning it. He and his wife and kids returned Sunday night exhausted instead of rested.

While nature and beauty are nice if they're available, they are not necessary for the Christian person who wants to quiet his or her soul to listen for the voice of God. Solitude, as the late theologian and writer Henri Nouwen wrote, is simply creating space for God. That means carving out time in our schedule to be quiet, to listen actively for God to speak to our spirit.

So often during times of solitude, I don't sense God speak. Nothing seems to happen. My mind always wanders. But as I've created space for solitude, I've discovered its real benefit is that during the day, my spiritual radar has gradually become more sensitive to the things of God. Even in the midst of a stressful, fast-paced day, I can detect the gentle impressions of the Holy Spirit.

–David L. Goetz

SOMETHING TO THINK ABOUT

Every character of great spiritual development in Scripture is marked by solitude.

—

John Ortberg

LOVE FOR THE OUTCAST

THE PERSON WE DESPISE MOST MAY BE THE PERSON GOD WANTS US TO REACH MOST.
THE "GOOD SAMARITAN" PARABLE IS SO FAMILIAR THAT WE CAN FORGET HOW MUCH
THE JEWS DESPISED THE HALF-BREED PEOPLE OF SAMARIA. JESUS INTENTIONALLY
MADE A SAMARITAN THE HERO OF THE STORY TO UNDERSCORE HIS POINT THAT OUR
POSITION IN SOCIETY IS MUCH LESS IMPORTANT THAN OUR ACTIONS TOWARD OTHERS.

LUKE 10:30–37

Jesus said: "A man was going down from Jerusalem to Jericho, when he fell into the hands of robbers. They stripped him of his clothes, beat him and went away, leaving him half dead. A priest happened to be going down the same road, and when he saw the man, he passed by on the other side. So too, a Levite, when he came to the place and saw him, passed by on the other side. But a Samaritan, as he traveled, came where the man was; and when he saw him, he took pity on him.

He went to him and bandaged his wounds, pouring on oil and wine. Then he put the man on his own donkey, took him to an inn and took care of him. The next day he took out two silver coins and gave them to the innkeeper. 'Look after him,' he said, 'and when I return, I will reimburse you for any extra expense you may have.'

"Which of these three do you think was a neighbor to the man who fell into the hands of robbers?"

The expert in the law replied, "The one who had mercy on him."

CHARACTER CHECK
Who in my life might be like the man the Samaritan stopped to help?

_____

_____

_____

_____

_____

IN BUSINESS TERMS

I was on a plane coming from Chicago to Milwaukee. I asked for a seat with an empty seat beside it, because I had a writing assignment, and I needed to spread out my Bible and notes, and study. So on this small plane, I ended up the only person with an empty seat next to her.

I got out my Bible, and just as we were about to take off, into the plane came this huge man, 6'4" or 6'5"–very masculine. But he was dressed like a woman–mini-skirt and stockings, high-heeled white shoes and purse, and wig. As this cross-dresser came down the aisle, I realized, *The only open seat is next to me. He's going to be sitting next to me all during this flight.* And I suddenly wanted to put my Bible away. I'm amazed I had these reactions. Prejudices I didn't know I had came out. I said to the Lord, "I don't really care about him. I really don't care if he goes to heaven or hell. And that's the truth. I'm writing and preaching about these things, and suddenly here is a real-life human being, and I don't care a bit about him."

I repented and said, "I'm sorry, Lord. Forgive me, and give me your heart for this man. You died for him."

I didn't lead him to Christ, but I smiled at him and changed my attitude. I began to ask myself, *What's happened in his life to bring him to this point?* At the end of the journey, I had a compassion for him I didn't have at the beginning.

–Jill Briscoe

SOMETHING TO THINK ABOUT

Let my heart be broken by the things that break the heart of God.

—

Bob Pierce

BEING BEFORE DOING

OUR CULTURE OFTEN DEFINES US BY WHAT WE DO. BUT SCRIPTURE CONSISTENTLY PLACES "BEING" BEFORE "DOING." THE STORY LUKE TELLS IS AN EXAMPLE. WE'RE TEMPTED TO GIVE MARTHA HIGH MARKS FOR HER WORK ETHIC. BUT JESUS OBSERVED THAT SHE COULD HAVE CHOSEN A BETTER OPTION.

LUKE 10:38–42

As Jesus and his disciples were on their way, he came to a village where a woman named Martha opened her home to him. She had a sister called Mary, who sat at the Lord's feet listening to what he said. But Martha was distracted by all the preparations that had to be made. She came to him and asked, "Lord, don't you care that my sister has left me to do the work by myself? Tell her to help me!"

"Martha, Martha," the Lord answered, "you are worried and upset about many things, but only one thing is needed. Mary has chosen what is better, and it will not be taken away from her."

CHARACTER CHECK
Which kind of explorer am I?

_____
_____
_____
_____
_____

IN BUSINESS TERMS

Phillips Brooks, a popular nineteenth-century preacher, said there are two kinds of explorers: One has to go over the mountains to take possession of the new frontier he's never seen before. The other kind of explorer becomes familiar with his or her own land and digs deeper and deeper into it.

The higher ambition is entering into the deeper possession of what we already have rather than going out to acquire something new.

Some Christians seem to need to go out and acquire more and more prestige or power. Others enter deeper into the character God has given them and pay more attention to the kind of people they're becoming.

I wonder: shouldn't ambition for the latter be held with at least as much esteem as the former? We don't have to always go on to bigger and better enterprises.

–Richard Nelson Bolles

SOMETHING TO THINK ABOUT

Character is that which can do without success.

—

Ralph Waldo Emerson

DIVINE URGENCY

GOD WEEPS OVER YOUR UNSAVED BUSINESS COLLEAGUE. JESUS TELLS OF THE SHEP-
HERD SEARCHING FOR THE ONE LOST SHEEP OUT OF A HUNDRED AND OF THE FATHER
WELCOMING HIS WAYWARD SON HOME. JESUS ALSO TELLS OF THE WOMAN WHO
SEARCHES FOR LOST COINS, EACH WORTH ABOUT A DAY'S WAGE. THERE IS AN
URGENCY TO GOD'S SEARCH FOR EACH PERSON.

LUKE 15:4–10

"Suppose one of you has a hundred sheep and loses one of them. Does he not leave the ninety-nine in the open country and go after the lost sheep until he finds it? And when he finds it, he joyfully puts it on his shoulders and goes home. Then he calls his friends and neighbors together and says, 'Rejoice with me; I have found my lost sheep.' I tell you that in the same way there will be more rejoicing in heaven over one sinner who repents than over ninety-nine righteous persons who do not need to repent.

"Or suppose a woman has ten silver coins and loses one. Does she not light a lamp, sweep the house and search carefully until she finds it? And when she finds it, she calls her friends and neighbors together and says, 'Rejoice with me; I have found my lost coin.' In the same way, I tell you, there is rejoicing in the presence of the angels of God over one sinner who repents."

CHARACTER CHECK

What is my natural approach to evangelism?

_____

_____

_____

_____

_____

IN BUSINESS TERMS

Christians can be hindered by traditional ideas of what evangelism looks like. The average Christian thinks, *It means getting out and knocking on doors. I don't know if I can do that.* We would like to reach lost people, but doing so doesn't feel like us.

In the New Testament, Peter was confrontational, while Paul took an intellectual approach. The blind man in John 9 took a testimonial approach, and the woman at the well, an invitational approach. So let's free ourselves up. Let's not lay guilt trips on people by acting as though if they really loved Jesus, they would do it just like us. Let's find approaches that fit the personalities God gave each of us.

Evangelism naturally tends to slip more than any other biblical value. It is what I call the law of evangelistic entropy. I've been negatively surprised by how rapidly this value slips, even in people who are fired up to share their faith. A year passes, and they've slipped into comfortable Christianity.

Denominations that started with evangelism as a priority can quickly become institutionalized. Evangelism is too often relegated to a statement on the front of a bulletin instead of a value by which we live.

–Mark Mittelberg

SOMETHING TO THINK ABOUT

The gospel must be preached afresh and told in new ways to every generation, since every generation has its own unique questions. The gospel must constantly be forwarded to a new address, because the recipient is repeatedly changing his place of residence.
—Helmut Thielicke

STANDING TALL FOR TRUTH

"BUT AREN'T THERE MANY WAYS TO GOD?" CHRISTIANS WHO SHARE THEIR FAITH WITH CO-WORKERS OR EXTENDED FAMILY OFTEN RUN INTO THIS QUESTION. IN TODAY'S WORLD, "INTOLERANCE" SEEMS TO BE THE GREATEST SIN. FORTIFIED BY PRAYER, GOD'S WORD, AND THE SUPPORT OF OTHER BELIEVERS, WE CAN STAND FIRM IN OUR CLAIMS FOR CHRIST.

JOHN 14:1–6

"Do not let your hearts be troubled. Trust in God; trust also in me. In my Father's house are many rooms; if it were not so, I would have told you. I am going there to prepare a place for you. And if I go and prepare a place for you, I will come back and take you to be with me that you also may be where I am. You know the way to the place where I am going."

Thomas said to him, "Lord, we don't know where you are going, so how can we know the way?"

Jesus answered, "I am the way and the truth and the life. No one comes to the Father except through me. If you really knew me, you would know my Father as well. From now on, you do know him and have seen him."

CHARACTER CHECK
How can I take a stronger stand for the claims of Christ in my workplace?

_____

_____

_____

_____

_____

IN BUSINESS TERMS

At the universities I visit, the exclusivity of Christ is raised in every open forum–"How can you possibly talk about one God or one way when there are so many good options?"

Today, sensitivities are at an all-time high–and rightfully so. Tolerance of different races and religions has been lacking over the years. But pluralism has given way to relativism. Most of the intellectual elite of this country completely disavow the idea of absolute truth.

But we cannot go to the university with the attitude, "I'm here to deal with your tough questions. . . ." I often tell about my struggles as a teenager. My stated vulnerability gives me an entry point. But even with a hard-edged question, I answer with graciousness. I have to earn the right to be heard every time I get up to speak.

"I'm going to defend why Jesus Christ is the only way to God," I might say. "You may disagree with that, but if you do, make sure your arguments counter the arguments I'm now presenting to you."

One key is the willingness to say, "I'm not sure how well I will deal with what you're going to say, but give me a chance. I have struggled with these issues, as well."

–Ravi Zacharias

SOMETHING TO THINK ABOUT

Hard are the ways of truth, and rough to walk.

—

John Milton

CALL OF THE DEEP

IF JESUS HAD DONE A COST-BENEFIT ANALYSIS ON HIS "CAREER" PRIOR TO DYING ON THE CROSS, HE MIGHT NOT HAVE GONE TO THE CROSS. THREE YEARS WAS NOT ENOUGH TIME TO SAVE THE WORLD. HE NEEDED AT LEAST ANOTHER THIRTY YEARS. YET JESUS HAD A DEEP SENSE THAT HE HAD FULFILLED WHAT GOD WANTED HIM TO DO. AS A RESULT, HE SAVED THE WORLD.

JOHN 17:4–5; 19:28–30

"I have brought you glory on earth by completing the work you gave me to do. And now, Father, glorify me in your presence with the glory I had with you before the world began...."

Later, knowing that all was now completed, and so that the Scripture would be fulfilled, Jesus said, "I am thirsty." A jar of wine vinegar was there, so they soaked a sponge in it, put the sponge on a stalk of the hyssop plant, and lifted it to Jesus' lips. When he had received the drink, Jesus said, "It is finished." With that, he bowed his head and gave up his spirit.

CHARACTER CHECK
Who has God called me to be–and to do with my remaining years?

_____

_____

_____

_____

_____

IN BUSINESS TERMS

"It is finished." According to John, these were the last words of Jesus. But what exactly was finished?

He was but a young man with many years of ministry ahead of him. He had been preaching for only three years and had little to show for it: the last of his followers had fled in fear; the kingdom of Rome seemed in no way threatened by the kingdom of God; recovery of sight hadn't yet come to many of the blind; captives were still doing time; liberty had not yet come to the underside of society.

Nothing much was finished, except that which God had called Jesus to do. "I glorified you on earth," Jesus prayed, "by finishing the work that you gave me to do."

It must have been tempting for him to try to do more, to try to, well, save the world. A few more years and who knows? Perhaps thousands more could be exposed to the kingdom's message; at least hundreds more could be touched by its healing power.

If he were like most of us, he would have let Peter go through with his rescue attempt–anything to get back to ministry, to continue his work. To the end, though, he refused to take responsibility for everything–to do what really mattered. For that reason, he did save the world.

Every leader must ask, "What am I called to do? Where should I invest my time and energies?"

–Donald McCullough

_____

_____

_____

_____

_____

DARE TO ENCOURAGE

THERE ARE A NUMBER OF GREAT JOSEPHS IN THE BIBLE—JOSEPH SON OF JACOB, WHO FORGAVE HIS BROTHERS; JOSEPH IN THE GOSPELS, WHO STOOD BY MARY; JOSEPH OF ARIMATHEA, WHO PROVIDED THE TOMB FOR OUR LORD'S BODY. BUT THERE'S ANOTHER JOSEPH, LESS WELL KNOWN. THE BOOK OF ACTS USUALLY CALLS HIM BY HIS NICKNAME, BARNABAS (SEE ACTS 4:36). BARNABAS MEANS "SON OF ENCOURAGEMENT."

ACTS 9:23–28

After many days had gone by, the Jews conspired to kill him, but Saul learned of their plan. Day and night they kept close watch on the city gates in order to kill him. But his followers took him by night and lowered him in a basket through an opening in the wall.

When [Saul] came to Jerusalem, he tried to join the disciples, but they were all afraid of him, not believing that he really was a disciple. But Barnabas took him and brought him to the apostles. He told them how Saul on his journey had seen the Lord and that the Lord had spoken to him, and how in Damascus he had preached fearlessly in the name of Jesus. So Saul stayed with them and moved about freely in Jerusalem, speaking boldly in the name of the Lord.

CHARACTER CHECK
Whom have I encouraged lately?

_____

_____

_____

_____

_____

IN BUSINESS TERMS

When I was governor, every few weeks I would have the name George Smoka on my calendar. He would come for the Union Gospel Mission and say with his commanding voice, "I've just come to pray for you, Brother." With that he would raise his one hand toward the heavens and place the other on my shoulder, and he would simply pray. Then he'd say, "Good-bye; have a good day, Brother." He'd walk out, and that was the extent of his call.

I always felt absolutely renewed and blessed by those calls. I think 90 percent of the people who called at my office were there for some request. But George Smoka never asked for a thing. That kind of humble support is invaluable for leaders.

Humility is unconscious. If you're conscious of your humility, it isn't true humility. Humility is a manner, a viewpoint, an all-encompassing thing.

But humility is expressed through actions, say, a nod of the head in acknowledgment of a verbal hello. It can be demonstrated simply by stopping and listening to someone. Its essence is putting others ahead of yourself. By God's grace it can be demonstrated by anyone in any position.

–Mark O. Hatfield

SOMETHING TO THINK ABOUT

The deepest principle in human nature is the craving to be appreciated.

—

William James

GOD'S CALL, OUR ACTIONS

Consumers want choices. Options allow customers to pick what is best for them. When it comes to picking a direction in life, however, too many options can paralyze us. Especially when facing major forks in the road, we desperately want to hear clearly from God. We don't want to pick the wrong option. But we may be missing the point.

ACTS 16:6–10

Paul and his companions traveled throughout the region of Phrygia and Galatia, having been kept by the Holy Spirit from preaching the word in the province of Asia. When they came to the border of Mysia, they tried to enter Bithynia, but the Spirit of Jesus would not allow them to. So they passed by Mysia and went down to Troas. During the night Paul had a vision of a man of Macedonia standing and begging him, "Come over to Macedonia and help us." After Paul had seen the vision, we got ready at once to leave for Macedonia, concluding that God had called us to preach the gospel to them.

CHARACTER CHECK

In what area in my life do I need to get moving, so I can know God better?

_____

_____

_____

_____

_____

IN BUSINESS TERMS

Several years after I graduated from high school, I bumped into a high-school classmate working construction. I asked him if he planned to go to college, and he said no. "I've decided it's a waste of time and money to go to college," he said, "when I don't know what I want to do with my life." Today, many years later, he is still working construction.

There's a saying that "God can't move a stone." Some think they have to wait to take action until God calls them. But God moves people who are already moving. He calls them during periods of activity, not when they're sitting around waiting for a sign. The apostle Paul and his companions were not idly wondering what to do next. They pursued plans to engage in missionary work in Asia when God called them to Macedonia.

I'll never forget what one of my mentors, a successful entrepreneur nearing retirement, said to me about his drive to succeed: "Reaching the top is not all it's cracked up to be. I learned I was more motivated by the work it took to achieve success than the success itself."

The principle is that the journey that forces us to pray and seek God's will is probably more important than the moment we discover God's will. Our destination is not so much to find the perfect plan for our life on earth; it's getting to know God along the way.

–David L. Goetz

SOMETHING TO THINK ABOUT

The place God calls you to is the place where your deep gladness and the world's deep hunger meet.

—

Frederick Buechner

WEIGHING OPTIONS

Few decisions in life are clear-cut. In fact, the art of decision-making is the skill of choosing between two goods. The apostle Paul faced a number of decisions in his ministry that were more mundane than moral. Even a Spirit-filled man like Paul had to weigh options and issues in order to make the best possible decision.

ACTS 19:21–23; 20:1–3

After all this had happened, Paul decided to go to Jerusalem, passing through Macedonia and Achaia. "After I have been there," he said, "I must visit Rome also." He sent two of his helpers, Timothy and Erastus, to Macedonia, while he stayed in the province of Asia a little longer. About that time there arose a great disturbance about the Way. . . .

When the uproar had ended, Paul sent for the disciples and, after encouraging them, said good-bye and set out for Macedonia. He traveled through that area, speaking many words of encouragement to the people, and finally arrived in Greece, where he stayed three months. Because the Jews made a plot against him just as he was about to sail for Syria, he decided to go back through Macedonia.

CHARACTER CHECK
What decisions am I facing that need more thought?

_____

_____

_____

_____

_____

IN BUSINESS TERMS

Many Christian leaders are handicapped because they almost inevitably think in moralistic terms only: rightness versus wrongness. "What's the right thing to do? What ought to be done?"

I keep reminding leaders there are other modes to consider: effective versus ineffective, good versus best, safe versus risky.

Virtually every decision has a moral aspect, either in its consequences or in the way the decision will be implemented. And most of us carry an intuitive desire to reach for the godly, to hear the words of God on a given issue and line up with him rather than against him. But not all church administration deals with Mount Sinai issues. Many decisions are more mundane and subtle.

Questions leaders need to be asking are: "What are my options? Who should be involved in the decision-making process? How do I know when I have enough information? When is it time to bite the bullet and decide?"

These are the questions that aren't asked often enough.

–Carl F. George

_____

_____

_____

_____

_____

ULTIMATE WORTH

WHAT MAKES YOU FEEL "WORTHY"? YOUR REPUTATION AMONG YOUR PROFESSIONAL PEERS, THE PERFORMANCE OF YOUR BUSINESS IN THE LAST QUARTER, THE NUMBER OF APPOINTMENTS IN YOUR CALENDAR? PAUL WAS A ROMAN CITIZEN, WHICH ACCORDED HIM SPECIAL STATUS IN THE SOCIETY OF HIS TIME. BUT HE KNEW THAT ONLY IN CHRIST DO WE FIND TRUE WORTH.

ROMANS 5:6–11

You see, at just the right time, when we were still powerless, Christ died for the ungodly. Very rarely will anyone die for a righteous man, though for a good man someone might possibly dare to die. But God demonstrates his own love for us in this: While we were still sinners, Christ died for us.

Since we have now been justified by his blood, how much more shall we be saved from God's wrath through him! For if, when we were God's enemies, we were reconciled to him through the death of his Son, how much more, having been reconciled, shall we be saved through his life! Not only is this so, but we also rejoice in God through our Lord Jesus Christ, through whom we have now received reconciliation.

CHARACTER CHECK

What can I do today as a response to God's incredible gift to me?

_____

_____

_____

_____

_____

IN BUSINESS TERMS

In ego we establish our worth. In the Christian context we let God establish our worth. How does he establish our worth? First, he made us unique; then he died for us. This fact is incomprehensible. I cannot grasp that Christ, the son of God, died for me. I can intellectually tell you that God died for me, but I cannot comprehend it. If I could, it would absolutely revolutionize my self-image.

If the President of the United States offered to die for me, I would expect to be interviewed by every member of the media and asked why and how it was to happen, and so forth. That would just be on his offer to die. If he actually were willing, his mentality would be checked out; there would be weeks of psychological studies on him and then there would be all kinds of studies on me. It would be one of the great events of history–that a president was willing to die for one of the citizens.

That is the same concept when we talk about God dying for man. It's too big to comprehend. Even if we had an inkling of it, it would give us self-worth.

Egomania–horizontal tension–gives relative value; Christianity–vertical tension–gives absolute value.

–Fred Smith, Sr.

SOMETHING TO THINK ABOUT

Nothing fails quite so totally as success without God.

—

Vic Pentz

REALLY LISTENING

LIFE NEVER WORKS LIKE IT'S SUPPOSED TO. IN ROMANS 8 THE APOSTLE PAUL DESCRIBED THE STRUGGLE FACED BY EVERYONE LIVING ON PLANET EARTH—SUFFERING, GROANING, BONDAGE, AND DECAY. BUT THE CHRISTIAN HAS HOPE. WE HAVE "PHASE ONE" BENEFITS (THE JOY OF KNOWING CHRIST IN THIS LIFE), BUT WE WAIT FOR SOMETHING GREATER IN THE LIFE TO COME.

ROMANS 8:18–25

I consider that our present sufferings are not worth comparing with the glory that will be revealed in us. The creation waits in eager expectation for the sons of God to be revealed. For the creation was subjected to frustration, not by its own choice, but by the will of the one who subjected it, in hope that the creation itself will be liberated from its bondage to decay and brought into the glorious freedom of the children of God.

We know that the whole creation has been groaning as in the pains of childbirth right up to the present time. Not only so, but we ourselves, who have the firstfruits of the Spirit, groan inwardly as we wait eagerly for our adoption as sons, the redemption of our bodies. For in this hope we were saved. But hope that is seen is no hope at all. Who hopes for what he already has? But if we hope for what we do not yet have, we wait for it patiently.

CHARACTER CHECK
How is the search for meaning expressed in my colleagues?

_____

_____

_____

_____

_____

IN BUSINESS TERMS

At every university where I've lectured, the intellectual questions eventually turn into questions of meaning. Often behind a difficult or angry question is a hurting heart; the intellect is intertwined with the heart. I always try to rescue a question from mere academic connotations.

Once a couple approached me after a church service and began asking questions about the problem of evil. As I began to answer their questions, I happened to glance at their baby, who had Downs Syndrome. Seeing their child, I had a new appreciation for their questions and the context behind them.

Nothing is as offensive as answers perceived to be mere words, uncaring of a human situation.

Even though the search for meaning is debunked today, it is still rigorously pursued. The postmodern world is still a world where technology and means play a greater role than people and relationships. But the cries of the human heart can be smothered only so long. And in these yearnings, the search for significance and fulfillment continues.

–Ravi Zacharias

CLIENTS IN NEED

YOUR INVESTMENT CLUB IS YOUR MISSION FIELD. SO IS YOUR GOLFING FOURSOME. AND THE DEPARTMENT YOU SUPERVISE AT WORK. THAT IS THE MESSAGE OF THE APOSTLE PAUL'S CHALLENGE TO BELIEVERS TO PREACH THE GOOD NEWS. WHEREVER YOU ARE, GOD WANTS YOU TO TELL OTHERS ABOUT HIM.

ROMANS 10:9–15

That if you confess with your mouth, "Jesus is Lord," and believe in your heart that God raised him from the dead, you will be saved. For it is with your heart that you believe and are justified, and it is with your mouth that you confess and are saved. As the Scripture says, "Anyone who trusts in him will never be put to shame." For there is no difference between Jew and Gentile–the same Lord is Lord of all and richly blesses all who call on him, for, "Everyone who calls on the name of the Lord will be saved."

How, then, can they call on the one they have not believed in? And how can they believe in the one of whom they have not heard? And how can they hear without someone preaching to them? And how can they preach unless they are sent? As it is written, "How beautiful are the feet of those who bring good news!"

CHARACTER CHECK
Who among my friends and colleagues might be open to the things of God?

_____

_____

_____

_____

_____

IN BUSINESS TERMS

Sometimes in [evangelism] we try to assume the Holy Spirit's role, but the much greater problem is our hoping the Holy Spirit will do our job for us. One popular version of evangelism says, "If I just live as a consistent Christian, people will see it, figure it out, and come to Christ." But that approach isn't biblical, and it doesn't work. In Romans 10:14 Paul said we have to go and give people the message. We have to initiate conversations and trust that the Holy Spirit will work as we bring the message to them.

Another temptation is to ride on the positive experience people have when they come to a church program and think they will be interested enough in what they've seen to figure it all out on their own.

Years ago a girl I knew from high school started coming to a Bible study I was leading. She learned the songs and started talking like us and hanging out with us. One day I said to her, "I'm glad you're part of our group."

"I love it," she said.

"Have you ever come to the point of committing your life to Christ so you know you're forgiven of your sins?"

"No, I've never done that," she said, "and no one ever told me I needed to."

We have to keep spelling out the basics.

–Mark Mittelberg

_____

_____

_____

_____

_____

WHERE CREDIT IS DUE

FEW SUCCESSES AT WORK ARE ACHIEVED WITHOUT A TEAM. EVEN IN THE MOST INDIVIDUALIS-
TIC SPORTS EVENTS, SUCH AS TRACK AND FIELD, THOSE WHO EXCEL HAVE COACHES, TRAINERS,
AND BENEFACTORS. WE OFTEN THINK OF THE APOSTLE PAUL AS A ONE-MAN SHOW, BUT IF
YOU PAY ATTENTION TO HIS LETTERS, YOU NOTICE JUST HOW MANY PEOPLE WORKED WITH
HIM. HE RELIED HEAVILY ON HIS FAR-FLUNG "TEAM."

ROMANS 16:1–4, 6–7, 13

*I commend to you our sister Phoebe, a servant of the church in
Cenchrea. I ask you to receive her in the Lord in a way worthy of the
saints and to give her any help she may need from you, for she has been
a great help to many people, including me.*

*Greet Priscilla and Aquila, my fellow workers in Christ Jesus. They
risked their lives for me. Not only I but all the churches of the Gentiles
are grateful to them. . . .*

*Greet Mary, who worked very hard for you. Greet Andronicus and
Junias, my relatives who have been in prison with me. They are out-
standing among the apostles, and they were in Christ before I was. . . .*

*Greet Rufus, chosen in the Lord, and his mother, who has been a
mother to me, too.*

CHARACTER CHECK
Am I developing leaders around me? How can I show appreciation to them?

IN BUSINESS TERMS

Dictators do not develop strong leaders for succession.

Once I was asked if I'd be interested in becoming president of a manufacturing corporation whose long-term dictatorial leader had recently died. I knew my team approach would not be profitable, for the subordinates had been taught to act on orders, not to think through solutions. I couldn't in good conscience ask people who hadn't taken responsibility for years to begin to think for themselves. The corporation needed a younger dictator to keep the company successful.

Historically, a benevolent dictator with great ability is the most efficient leader for most organizations over the time of his service. Long term, however, he is frequently a detriment to the health of the organization after he leaves.

In corporate management I was taught that the perpetuation of healthy organization is management's first responsibility, and so leadership development at all levels is of prime importance. Successful succession is a leader's responsibility and often a test of his character.

–Fred Smith, Sr.

SOMETHING TO THINK ABOUT

Three helping one another will do as much as six men singly.

—

Spanish proverb

BEYOND THE PACKAGING

"IMAGE IS NOTHING; THIRST IS EVERYTHING" WAS AN ADVERTISING SLOGAN FOR A POPULAR SODA "IMAGE IS NOTHING; CHARACTER IS EVERYTHING"—DESCRIBES THE APOSTLE PAUL. PAUL WAS NOT MUCH TO LOOK AT AND NOT AN IMPRESSIVE SPEAKER. THANKFULLY, THE EARLY CHURCH CARED MORE ABOUT PAUL'S CHARACTER THAN HIS PRESENTATION.

1 CORINTHIANS 2:1–5, 12–13

When I came to you, brothers, I did not come with eloquence or superior wisdom as I proclaimed to you the testimony about God. For I resolved to know nothing while I was with you except Jesus Christ and him crucified. I came to you in weakness and fear, and with much trembling. My message and my preaching were not with wise and persuasive words, but with a demonstration of the Spirit's power, so that your faith might not rest on men's wisdom, but on God's power. . . .

We have not received the spirit of the world but the Spirit who is from God, that we may understand what God has freely given us. This is what we speak, not in words taught us by human wisdom but in words taught by the Spirit, expressing spiritual truths in spiritual words.

CHARACTER CHECK
How have I focused on my character development in recent years?

_____

_____

_____

_____

IN BUSINESS TERMS

Recently I heard a marvelous missionary speaker, a woman who had served in the jungles of an equatorial country for almost forty years. She had a somewhat dowdy appearance; she wasn't dressed in the latest styles. Her hairdo was a little out of fashion, and she was not a particularly polished speaker. She shuffled her notes a few times and looked for a couple of quotes she'd lost in her notebook. She spoke quietly and humbly.

But I was so invigorated and challenged. She told stories of how she and her husband took their small children into jungles where malaria was running rampant, where rivers were infested with crocodiles, where the monsoon rains came down, and where their tiny grass hut, up on twenty-foot pilings of bamboo, was shaking in the wind. The natives they were trying to reach were cannibals who practiced headhunting.

The fact that she wasn't a polished speaker made her stories and insights from God's Word all the more brilliant. They shined with a kind of unpolished glory. Her speaking was so unmanmade, so divine.

Unfortunately, not everyone in the audience was so impressed. It made me wonder, can we not rely on the Word of God or the Spirit of God to enable us to look at somebody through the light of his grace and see character, perseverance, self-control, self-discipline, a desire to obey?

–Joni Eareckson Tada

SOMETHING TO THINK ABOUT

Common-looking people are the best in the world: that is the reason the Lord makes so many of them.

—

Abraham Lincoln

FAITHFUL TO THE END

LEADERS TEND TO THINK BIG—BIG PLANS, BIG ACCOMPLISHMENTS. THE DANGER IS
THAT WITH THIS MINDSET, WE CAN SET OURSELVES UP FOR FRUSTRATION WHEN THE
RESULTS FALL SHORT OF OUR VISION. BUT A RECURRING, AND REASSURING, THEME
OF THE BIBLE IS THAT GOD HONORS AND USES EVEN THE SMALLEST EFFORT.
FAITHFULNESS IS OUR BUSINESS; RESULTS ARE GOD'S.

1 CORINTHIANS 4:1-5

*So then, men ought to regard us as servants of Christ and as those
entrusted with the secret things of God. Now it is required that those
who have been given a trust must prove faithful. I care very little if I am
judged by you or by any human court; indeed, I do not even judge
myself. My conscience is clear, but that does not make me innocent. It
is the Lord who judges me. Therefore judge nothing before the appointed time; wait till the Lord comes. He will bring to light what is hidden
in darkness and will expose the motives of men's hearts. At that time
each will receive his praise from God .*

CHARACTER CHECK
If God rewards my small efforts, can I do the same with others?

_____

_____

_____

_____

_____

IN BUSINESS TERMS

I know that my suffering is "successful" when I am faithful to Christ in it. I'm choosing to be obedient, even if it's a drastic, small obedience that goes against the grain of my nature.

Being faithful to him, even when there are no evidences of joy or peace or blessing or camaraderie of spirit with other Christians, is the measure of success.

Recently my pastor and I were reminding each other how grateful we are that when we go to be with the Lord Jesus, he's going to say, "Well done, good and faithful servant! You have been faithful with a few things. I will put you in charge of many things."

How incredible that is–God thinks exponentially! If we've been faithful in a teeny, tiny, small matter, then God uses not arithmetic but trigonometry; he multiplies it a hundredfold. How good of God to do that based not on our success but our faithfulness and our mission. God will never do a cost-benefit analysis of our ministry.

–Joni Eareckson Tada

SOMETHING TO THINK ABOUT

If a man is to be called a street sweeper, he should sweep streets even as Michelangelo painted, or Beethoven composed music, or Shakespeare wrote poetry. He should sweep streets so well that all the hosts of heaven and earth will pause to say, "Here lived a great street sweeper who did his job well."

—

Martin Luther King, Jr.

DIVERSE BY DESIGN

THE DICTATOR-APPROACH TO MANAGEMENT IS THE MOST EFFICIENT, BUT IN THE
LONG TERM IT'S THE LEAST EFFECTIVE. SO OFTEN IT SEEMS EASIER TO DO THINGS
OURSELVES; WE WISH WE DIDN'T HAVE TO DEAL WITH SO MANY VARYING PERSONALI-
TIES, AGENDAS, AND DIVERSE WAYS OF SEEING LIFE. BUT BY DESIGN, DIVERSITY IS
PART OF THE GENETIC CODE OF THE BODY OF CHRIST.

1 CORINTHIANS 12:4-7, 11-14

*There are different kinds of gifts, but the same Spirit. There are dif-
ferent kinds of service, but the same Lord. There are different kinds of
working, but the same God works all of them in all men. Now to each
one the manifestation of the Spirit is given for the common good. . . .*

*All these are the work of one and the same Spirit, and he gives
them to each one, just as he determines.*

*The body is a unit, though it is made up of many parts; and though
all its parts are many, they form one body. So it is with Christ. For we
were all baptized by one Spirit into one body--whether Jews or Greeks,
slave or free--and we were all given the one Spirit to drink. Now the
body is not made up of one part but of many.*

CHARACTER CHECK
Am I tolerant of the diversity within the body of Christ?

_____

_____

_____

_____

_____

IN BUSINESS TERMS

Ephesians 1:9-10 is God's agenda for uniting all things in Christ. I also think of the passage in Ephesians 4, where Paul says that when Christ ascended he left gifts: apostles, prophets, evangelists, pastors, and teachers to equip the saints for works of ministry until we all reach unity and become mature in the fullness of the stature of Christ. Then we will not be tossed about by every wind of teaching, but will speak the truth in love, growing up into Christ.

If I am taking my call seriously as a servant of Jesus Christ, that's my agenda, and I must be about unity, not conformity. Diversity is essential to unity. I can't imagine a painting that is all one color.

The issue is Jesus Christ, and if a person honors Christ, then that person is a brother or a sister, and we can have fellowship regardless of other differences.

–Richard Halverson

SOMETHING TO THINK ABOUT

If two people agree on everything, you may be sure that one of them is doing all the thinking.

—

Anonymous

FINDING YOUR STRENGTHS

"WHAT ARE YOU GOING TO BE WHEN YOU GROW UP?" A LOT OF PEOPLE IN MIDLIFE ARE STILL ASKING THEMSELVES THAT QUESTION. THE ANSWER TO THAT QUESTION, THOUGH, IS ANOTHER QUESTION: WHAT ARE YOUR STRENGTHS? IN THE NEW TESTAMENT, THE ASSUMPTION SEEMS TO BE THAT CHRISTIAN BELIEVERS WILL KNOW THEM OR TAKE THE EFFORT TO FIND OUT.

1 CORINTHIANS 12:13-20

For we were all baptized by one Spirit into one body–whether Jews or Greeks, slave or free–and we were all given the one Spirit to drink.

Now the body is not made up of one part but of many. If the foot should say, "Because I am not a hand, I do not belong to the body," it would not for that reason cease to be part of the body. And if the ear should say, "Because I am not an eye, I do not belong to the body," it would not for that reason cease to be part of the body. If the whole body were an eye, where would the sense of hearing be? If the whole body were an ear, where would the sense of smell be? But in fact God has arranged the parts in the body, every one of them, just as he wanted them to be. If they were all one part, where would the body be? As it is, there are many parts, but one body.

CHARACTER CHECK
As I look over the past ten years of my life, where have I seen results?

_____

_____

_____

_____

_____

IN BUSINESS TERMS

The key question for a leader is "What can I do in this organization that nobody else can do?" And several questions emerge from that: What did the good Lord ordain me for? What are my strengths? Where have I seen results?

Very few of us ask these questions because very few of us even know how we perform. What am I good at? We don't usually ask that question. We've been trained to notice our weaknesses, not our strengths.

Schools, of necessity, are remedial institutions. When teachers meet with parents, rarely do they say, "Your Johnny should do more writing. He's so talented in writing." No, more likely you'll hear, "Johnny needs more work on his math. He's a bit weak in that area."

As a result, few of us really know our strengths. The great teachers, and great leaders, recognize strengths and focus on them.

–Peter Drucker

SOMETHING TO THINK ABOUT

Those who know how to win are much more numerous than those who know how to make proper use out of their victories.

—

Polybius

CLAY POTS

ONE DANGER OF BUSINESS SUCCESS IS THAT IN OUR MINDS, WE BECOME LARGER THAN LIFE. ACCORDING TO 2 CORINTHIANS 4, THOUGH, SUCCESSFUL PEOPLE ARE ONLY CLAY POTS—GLORIFIED COOKINGWARE—IN WHICH GOD CHOOSES TO DISPLAY HIS POWER. IT'S IMPORTANT TO ACCEPT AND EVEN EMBRACE THIS TENSION—WE'RE CLAY POTS FULFILLING A DIVINE PURPOSE. ANY SUCCESS WE HAVE COMES FROM GOD.

2 CORINTHIANS 4:6-11

For God, who said, "Let light shine out of darkness," made his light shine in our hearts to give us the light of the knowledge of the glory of God in the face of Christ.

But we have this treasure in jars of clay to show that this all-surpassing power is from God and not from us. We are hard pressed on every side, but not crushed; perplexed, but not in despair; persecuted, but not abandoned; struck down, but not destroyed. We always carry around in our body the death of Jesus, so that the life of Jesus may also be revealed in our body. For we who are alive are always being given over to death for Jesus' sake, so that his life may be revealed in our mortal body.

CHARACTER CHECK

Who needs me to communicate to them warmth and compassion?

_____

_____

_____

_____

_____

IN BUSINESS TERMS

It's helpful to keep in touch with my humanity and to recognize that I talk a lot more than I do. I preach beyond what I am able to live. That gives me a sense of empathy and understanding with people who hear a lot more than they are able to perform, or are admonished to do more than they actually enact.

When I start from the level ground beneath the cross-acknowledging that we all are human and hold the treasure of the gospel in earthen vessels–I can be a much more creative motivator and actually talk about the distance between what we are and what we do.

My identification with people frees them to take the first step. When I see them not as recalcitrant children but as needy people who long to grow, I then have the ability to begin to touch their lives with Christ and help them bring themselves out of apathy.

–Lloyd John Ogilvie

SOMETHING TO THINK ABOUT

I always prefer to believe the best of everybody—it saves so much trouble.

—

Rudyard Kipling

FAITH IN THE DARKNESS

NOTHING DEVASTATES MORE THAN THE LOSS OF A CHILD. YET AT LIFE'S DARKEST
MOMENTS, OUR FAITH BECOMES MORE THAN A BELIEF, BUT A ROCK-HARD REALITY
ON WHICH TO HOLD. IN 2 CORINTHIANS 5 PAUL PROVIDES THE FOUNDATIONS FOR
THIS TRUTH: WE GRIEVE WITH THE ASSURANCE THAT SOMEDAY WE WILL BE
"AT HOME WITH THE LORD."

2 CORINTHIANS 5:1, 6-10

*Now we know that if the earthly tent we live in is destroyed, we
have a building from God, an eternal house in heaven, not built by
human hands....*

*Therefore we are always confident and know that as long as we are
at home in the body we are away from the Lord. We live by faith, not by
sight. We are confident, I say, and would prefer to be away from the
body and at home with the Lord. So we make it our goal to please him,
whether we are at home in the body or away from it. For we must all
appear before the judgment seat of Christ, that each one may receive
what is due him for the things done while in the body, whether good or
bad.*

CHARACTER CHECK
How much of my life do I live with an eye on eternity?

_____

_____

_____

_____

_____

IN BUSINESS TERMS

About a month after the funeral of my adult daughter, my wife and I were in Washington, D.C. On Saturday morning, as we headed for the elevator to go to breakfast, I thought, *I wonder what Susie's doing right now?* As quickly as I thought it, another thought hit me: *I know exactly where she is. I know exactly what she's doing.*

Every parent always wants to know where his or her children are, regardless of their age. I didn't have a clue where my other kids were, but I knew where Susie was. The joy in knowing she was fine, better than fine, was overwhelming.

I'm a born optimist; I'll take my last two dollars and buy a money belt with it. But there's a big difference between the joy of optimism and the joy that comes with knowing you're in God's will, that he has already won this deal. All I've got to do is collect. It's not what I do, it's what Christ did.

–Zig Ziglar

SOMETHING TO THINK ABOUT

We see heaven more clearly through the prism of tears.

—

Robertson McQuilkin

FROM PAIN TO PURPOSE

A BASIC LEADERSHIP PRINCIPLE SAYS, "GO WITH YOUR STRENGTHS"—TAKE WHAT YOU ALREADY DO WELL AND PUT EVEN MORE ENERGY INTO DEVELOPING IT. YET GOD SPECIALIZES IN USING OUR WEAKNESSES TO FURTHER HIS PURPOSES. THE APOSTLE PAUL HAD SOME SORT OF "THORN IN THE FLESH," LIKELY A PHYSICAL WEAKNESS THAT GOD USED TO TEACH PAUL TO DEPEND ON HIM.

2 CORINTHIANS 12:7-10

To keep me from becoming conceited because of these surpassingly great revelations, there was given me a thorn in my flesh, a messenger of Satan, to torment me. Three times I pleaded with the Lord to take it away from me. But he said to me, "My grace is sufficient for you, for my power is made perfect in weakness." Therefore I will boast all the more gladly about my weaknesses, so that Christ's power may rest on me. That is why, for Christ's sake, I delight in weaknesses, in insults, in hardships, in persecutions, in difficulties. For when I am weak, then I am strong.

CHARACTER CHECK
How has God used my weaknesses to further his ends?

_____

_____

_____

_____

_____

IN BUSINESS TERMS

I think life is supposed to be difficult. A lot of life is grabbing your leg by the calf, jerking it out of the earth, putting it down in front of you, and going onward.

With my disability, some days are easier than others. But for me, life is always difficult. These are issues I must face every single morning.

Every morning somebody has to give me a bath in bed, dress me, lift me into a wheelchair, comb my hair, brush my teeth, fix my breakfast, cut up my food, and feed me.

When it comes to the day-to-day routines of dealing with the paralysis, at worst, it's depressing; at best, it's boring. I can't live with those flat facts. I have to turn them, by God's grace, into something that has meaning and purpose.

–Joni Eareckson Tada

SOMETHING TO THINK ABOUT

He who can't endure the bad will not live to see the good.

—

Yiddish proverb

PLUGGING AWAY

MUCH OF LIFE BOILS DOWN TO PLUGGING ALONG—ON A TASK, ON A RELATIONSHIP. SPIRITUAL MATURITY, TOO, IS BUILT ON CONSISTENT FAITHFULNESS, EVEN WHEN WE DON'T SEE DRAMATIC EVIDENCE OF GOD'S WORKING IN OUR LIVES. THE WORLD VALUES INSTANT SUCCESS AND READY SOLUTIONS, BUT GOD TAKES A MUCH LONGER VIEW.

GALATIANS 6:7-9; HEBREWS 10:35-37, 39

Do not be deceived: God cannot be mocked. A man reaps what he sows. The one who sows to please his sinful nature, from that nature will reap destruction; the one who sows to please the Spirit, from the Spirit will reap eternal life. Let us not become weary in doing good, for at the proper time we will reap a harvest if we do not give up. . . .

So do not throw away your confidence; it will be richly rewarded. You need to persevere so that when you have done the will of God, you will receive what he has promised. For in just a very little while, "He who is coming will come and will not delay. . . ." But we are not of those who shrink back and are destroyed, but of those who believe and are saved.

CHARACTER CHECK
In what areas in my life am I tempted to quit?

_____

_____

_____

_____

_____

IN BUSINESS TERMS

In 1972 NASA launched the exploratory space probe Pioneer 10. According to Leon Jaroff in Time magazine, the satellite's primary mission was to reach Jupiter, photograph it and its moons, and beam data to earth about the planet's magnetic field, radiation belts, and atmosphere. Scientists regarded this as a bold plan because up until then no satellite had gone beyond Mars, and they feared the asteroid belt would destroy the satellite before it could reach its target.

But Pioneer 10 accomplished its mission and much more. Swinging past Jupiter in November 1973, the space probe was hurled at a higher rate of speed toward the edge of the solar system by the planet's immense gravity. At one billion miles from the sun, Pioneer 10 passed Saturn. At some two billion miles, it hurtled past Uranus; Neptune, at nearly three billion miles; Pluto, at almost four billion miles. By 1997, twenty-five years after its launch, Pioneer 10 was more than six billion miles from the sun. And despite that immense distance, Pioneer 10 continues to beam back radio signals to scientists on Earth.

"Perhaps most remarkable," writes Jaroff, "is that those signals emanate from an eight-watt transmitter, which radiates about as much power as a bedroom night-light, and takes more than nine hours to reach Earth."

Engineers designed Pioneer 10 with a useful life of only three years. By simple longevity, its tiny eight-watt transmitter radio has accomplished more than anyone thought possible. So it is when we offer ourselves to serve the Lord. God can work even through someone with eight-watt abilities.

–Craig Brian Larson

SOMETHING TO THINK ABOUT

Perseverance is a great element of success. If you only knock long enough and loudly enough at the gate, you are sure to wake up somebody.

—

Henry Wadsworth Longfellow

END OF THE BOTTOM LINE

THE IMPORTANCE OF THE BOTTOM LINE IS ONE OF THE FIRST LESSONS OF BUSINESS. EFFECTIVE BUSINESS AND PROFESSIONAL LEADERS ARE NATURALLY PERFORMANCE-ORIENTED. THEY UNDERSTAND THE NEED FOR RESULTS. BUT THAT ATTITUDE CAN SOMETIMES NEGATIVELY AFFECT OUR SPIRITUAL LIVES.

EPHESIANS 2:4-10

But because of his great love for us, God, who is rich in mercy, made us alive with Christ even when we were dead in transgressions—it is by grace you have been saved. And God raised us up with Christ and seated us with him in the heavenly realms in Christ Jesus, in order that in the coming ages he might show the incomparable riches of his grace, expressed in his kindness to us in Christ Jesus. For it is by grace you have been saved, through faith—and this not from yourselves, it is the gift of God—not by works, so that no one can boast. For we are God's workmanship, created in Christ Jesus to do good works, which God prepared in advance for us to do.

CHARACTER CHECK
How can I slow down to revel in what God has done for me?

_____

_____

_____

_____

_____

IN BUSINESS TERMS

While hiking alone out of the country, I crushed my left leg in a bad fall. I had to drag myself nearly three hours to get to a road, where miraculously I was found and taken to a hospital. Eventually I was flown back to the United States for surgery.

The most profound result of that accident was that I discovered God in my pain. There I was, stretched out in bed in excruciating pain, and praying didn't make the pain go away. So I began to ask God how to find him in the midst of the pain and not only as the alleviator of pain. He answered that prayer. Some of the times of deepest pain and anguish were periods of closest fellowship with him.

For the first time in my life, I was taken off the fast track for a brief time. I discovered most of my security and identity was in what I accomplished for God—preaching sermons, writing books, leading a church, being part of a media ministry. All of this identified my worth.

What can you do when there's nothing to do but wait for healing?

During that difficult convalescence, I discovered in a new way that God loves me not for what I do but simply because I belong to him.

–Lloyd John Ogilvie

SOMETHING TO THINK ABOUT

We can't save ourselves by pulling on our bootstraps, even when our bootstraps are made of the finest religious leather.

—

Eugene Peterson

_____

_____

_____

_____

_____

IDEAL TO LIVE OUT

ONLY THE CHURCH HAS THE TRUE BASIS FOR RACIAL UNITY. THE CHURCH IS AT ITS BEST WHEN PEOPLE WITH NOTHING IN COMMON ARE UNITED IN CHRIST. WHEN THE CHURCH FUNCTIONS WELL, IT PICTURES ETERNITY, WHEN FOREVER WE'LL LIVE IN HARMONY WITH PEOPLE OF ALL RACES. THIS IS THE BIBLICAL IDEAL—IT'S UP TO GOD'S PEOPLE TO LIVE IT OUT.

EPHESIANS 2:14–16, 19-21

For he himself is our peace, who has made the two one and has destroyed the barrier, the dividing wall of hostility, by abolishing in his flesh the law with its commandments and regulations. His purpose was to create in himself one new man out of the two, thus making peace, and in this one body to reconcile both of them to God through the cross, by which he put to death their hostility. . . .

Consequently, you are no longer foreigners and aliens, but fellow citizens with God's people and members of God's household, built on the foundation of the apostles and prophets, with Christ Jesus himself as the chief cornerstone. In him the whole building is joined together and rises to become a holy temple in the Lord.

CHARACTER CHECK

How can I respond to racial comments I hear around me?

_____

_____

_____

_____

_____

IN BUSINESS TERMS

I minister in a racially mixed church on the west side of Chicago. I attended a wedding not long ago of a family who lives in Nebraska. I remember standing on this farmer's front lawn and seeing only one road, no other people, and corn in every direction. The scene couldn't have been farther from the west side of Chicago. Yet this farmer has developed one of the closest relationships with the people of our community.

It began the day he arrived with a work crew some years ago. During that week, he got connected with people in the neighborhood, and all his stereotypes began to break down.

When he returned for a second visit, he told me: "The Monday after I came home from my first work trip to Chicago, I met with the same fellas I've been having coffee and a roll with for twenty-five years. But this time, I had to get up and leave, because the same jokes, the same conversation, the same prejudices that never bothered me before now got to me."

His daughter is now a staff member at our church.

–Glen Kehrein

SOMETHING TO THINK ABOUT

When a person of one race treats with contempt a person of another race, he is revealing weaknesses in his own character.

—

Wellington Boone

BUILDING LEADERS

EFFECTIVE DELEGATION INVOLVES DEVELOPING OTHERS. THAT PRINCIPLE IS AT WORK IN THE NEW TESTAMENT. ACCORDING TO EPHESIANS 4, GOD HAS GIVEN LEADERS TO THE CHURCH TO DEVELOP OTHERS, NOT TO DO ALL THE WORK THEMSELVES.

EPHESIANS 4:11-16

It was he who gave some to be apostles, some to be prophets, some to be evangelists, and some to be pastors and teachers, to prepare God's people for works of service, so that the body of Christ may be built up until we all reach unity in the faith and in the knowledge of the Son of God and become mature, attaining to the whole measure of the fullness of Christ.

Then we will no longer be infants, tossed back and forth by the waves, and blown here and there by every wind of teaching and by the cunning and craftiness of men in their deceitful scheming. Instead, speaking the truth in love, we will in all things grow up into him who is the Head, that is, Christ. From him the whole body, joined and held together by every supporting ligament, grows and builds itself up in love, as each part does its work.

CHARACTER CHECK
Who is someone I could begin investing myself in today?

_____

_____

_____

_____

_____

IN BUSINESS TERMS

Everywhere I've served, I've prayed for God to send me leaders to build his church. For fourteen years, at least once every month or so, I'd meet someone visiting [my former pastorate] Skyline Church for the first time. We'd introduce ourselves. Then God would speak to me and say, "John, there's one." That was the most humbling thing in life because I didn't do one thing to bring that person in.

After I resigned, I was with about seventy-five church leaders one night for a farewell dinner. I got up and said, "All my life I've prayed for leaders. Let me tell how God answered those prayers with you."

Then I went around the room, telling each one about the time I met them, when God revealed, "There's one."

By the time I was done, we were all bawling. Someone said, "How could you remember meeting everyone in a church this size?"

I replied, "I don't remember meeting every person. I remember meeting you because you were one of those people I prayed God would lead into my life."

If you pray for leaders; if you have a heart to develop, lead, and empower people; if you've got a God-given vision, God will give according to your heart's desires.

–John Maxwell

SOMETHING TO THINK ABOUT

Effective executives never ask, "How does he get along with me?" Their question is, "What does he contribute?" Their question is never, "What can a man not do?" Their question is always, "What can he do uncommonly well?"

—

Peter Drucker

BIGGER THAN CONFLICT

No organization has ever moved forward without conflict among its leaders. Conflict, while often painful, is inevitable. While we can't avoid conflict, we can grow through it, especially as we follow the apostle Paul's guidelines for handling differences with others.

EPHESIANS 4:25–27, 29-32

Therefore each of you must put off falsehood and speak truthfully to his neighbor, for we are all members of one body. "In your anger do not sin": Do not let the sun go down while you are still angry, and do not give the devil a foothold. . . .

Do not let any unwholesome talk come out of your mouths, but only what is helpful for building others up according to their needs, that it may benefit those who listen. And do not grieve the Holy Spirit of God, with whom you were sealed for the day of redemption.

Get rid of all bitterness, rage and anger, brawling and slander, along with every form of malice. Be kind and compassionate to one another, forgiving each other, just as in Christ God forgave you.

CHARACTER CHECK
How well do I handle conflict?

_____

_____

_____

_____

_____

IN BUSINESS TERMS

With the help of my wife, Christian counselors, and other trusted friends, I'm learning a more constructive way to negotiate conflict. I'm learning to admit to the person involved that what they said or did hurt me, and slowly I'm learning to feel that hurt inside. I'm learning to say "ouch" and talk about what that ouch means, rather than discounting relational wounds and powering past them.

As I get better at acknowledging the hurt that conflict causes me, I also become more aware of the hurt that conflict causes others. This has led me to approach conflict resolution with a much gentler spirit, both for my sake and for others' sake.

Bottom line, I'm talking about a kind of vulnerability in relationships that did not come naturally to me. But I really believe it's a necessary part of obedience to Christ.

–Bill Hybels

SOMETHING TO THINK ABOUT

Coping with difficult people is always a problem, especially if the difficult person happens to be yourself.

—

Anonymous

FAMILY VALUES

MARTYRED MISSIONARY JIM ELLIOT ONCE WROTE THAT HE THANKED GOD FOR A DAD WHO "[HAD] NOT SPENT SO MUCH TIME REARING OTHER PEOPLE'S CHILDREN THAT HE [HADN'T] HAD TIME FOR HIS OWN." THE PRESSURE OF WORK CAN PUSH THE PRIORITY OF FAMILY DOWN THE LIST. WHEN WE ALWAYS HAVE TO BE "ON" AT WORK, IT'S EASY TO LET DOWN AT HOME. YET SUCCESS AT HOME HAS ETERNAL VALUE.

EPHESIANS 5:25-29; 6:4

Husbands, love your wives, just as Christ loved the church and gave himself up for her to make her holy, cleansing her by the washing with water through the word, and to present her to himself as a radiant church, without stain or wrinkle or any other blemish, but holy and blameless. In this same way, husbands ought to love their wives as their own bodies. He who loves his wife loves himself. After all, no one ever hated his own body, but he feeds and cares for it, just as Christ does the church. . . .

Fathers, do not exasperate your children; instead, bring them up in the training and instruction of the Lord.

CHARACTER CHECK
What does my allocation of time say about my priorities?

_____

_____

_____

_____

_____

IN BUSINESS TERMS

The home is the toughest environment of all for leaders. Why is it the ones we love most are the ones we are most impatient with? My wife has often said to me, "I wish you were as patient with your children as you are with your constituents." She's right. She reminds me that I'm accountable to God and to my family, and I'm grateful for that.

I think the greatest problem is our allocation of time, whether we let our professions work to the exclusion of our families. If our lives are going to be given only to our professions, then better we had remained as Paul said, unencumbered by marriage and family. But if we do decide to marry and have a family, I am thoroughly convinced one has to set priorities as follows:

First to God. The Bible teaches us to "love the Lord your God with all your heart and with all your soul and with all your mind." Our second priority is to our families, because they are the gift of God to us; they are the joint effort of God's authority working through us. Our third priority is our professions, and if we put our jobs any place higher than third place, we have our priorities askew.

I've tried to communicate to my family that no matter how busy I am, I am always accessible to them. That has to be communicated verbally, but also in action.

–Mark Hatfield

SOMETHING TO THINK ABOUT

By profession I am a soldier and take pride in that fact. But I am prouder— infinitely prouder— to be a father.

—

Douglas MacArthur

CHINKS IN THE ARMOR

SATAN IS NOT STUPID. HE KNOWS EXACTLY WHAT OUR WEAKNESSES ARE, AND THAT'S WHERE HE TRIES TO PENETRATE OUR ARMOR. EPHESIANS REMINDS US THAT SATAN AND HIS AGENTS LURK BEHIND THE STRUGGLES WE FACE IN OUR LIVES—BUT ALSO THAT GOD GIVES US HIS WEAPONS.

EPHESIANS 6:13-18

Therefore put on the full armor of God, so that when the day of evil comes, you may be able to stand your ground, and after you have done everything, to stand. Stand firm then, with the belt of truth buckled round your waist, with the breastplate of righteousness in place, and with your feet fitted with the readiness that comes from the gospel of peace.

In addition to all this, take up the shield of faith, with which you can extinguish all the flaming arrows of the evil one. Take the helmet of salvation and the sword of the Spirit, which is the word of God. And pray in the Spirit on all occasions with all kinds of prayers and requests. With this in mind, be alert and always keep on praying for all the saints.

CHARACTER CHECK
Where am I most vulnerable to Satan's attacks?

_____

_____

_____

_____

_____

IN BUSINESS TERMS

Most of us don't know our weaknesses. We don't know where we're vulnerable. And that's where we get tripped up.

We've got to be realistic about the tactics of Satan. Paul says we are not to be ignorant of his devices. One translation renders it: "I'm up to his tricks."

And we must know how to draw on the resources God has given us, which means learning to put on the armor described in Ephesians 6.

Prayer is our support system. We are wise to lean on our spouses, colleagues, and Christian friends, asking them to pray for us and help us through. That's fellowship, and we are told, all of us, to live in fellowship. No Christian is meant to be a Lone Ranger, a self-sufficient hero, in the spiritual battle. We can't do it, and we shouldn't try.

–J. I. Packer

SOMETHING TO THINK ABOUT

We may not pay [Satan] reverence, for that would be indiscreet, but we can at least respect his talents.

—

Mark Twain

_____

_____

_____

_____

_____

CONFIDENCE IN TRUTH

THE PHRASE "ALWAYS CONFIDENT, SOMETIMES RIGHT" DESCRIBES A LOT OF PEOPLE IN BUSINESS, ESPECIALLY BOSSES. A TWIST ON THAT PHRASE— "ALWAYS CONFIDENT, ALWAYS RIGHT"—SHOULD BE APPLIED TO OUR ATTITUDE ABOUT SHARING THE GOSPEL. WE CAN BE CONFIDENT IN THE TRUTH OF THE GOSPEL AND IN THE HOLY SPIRIT'S ABILITY TO TAKE WHAT WE SAY AND CHANGE A LIFE.

PHILIPPIANS 1:19-26

[For] I know that through your prayers and the help given by the Spirit of Jesus Christ, what has happened to me will turn out for my deliverance. I eagerly expect and hope that I will in no way be ashamed, but will have sufficient courage so that now as always Christ will be exalted in my body, whether by life or by death. For to me, to live is Christ and to die is gain. If I am to go on living in the body, this will mean fruitful labor for me. Yet what shall I choose? I do not know! I am torn between the two: I desire to depart and be with Christ, which is better by far; but it is more necessary for you that I remain in the body. Convinced of this, I know that I will remain, and I will continue with all of you for your progress and joy in the faith, so that through my being with you again your joy in Christ Jesus will overflow on account of me.

CHARACTER CHECK
Is my confidence in the message of the gospel greater than in how I present it?

_____

_____

_____

_____

_____

IN BUSINESS TERMS

On July 15, 1986, Roger Clemens, the sizzling right-hander for the Boston Red Sox, started his first All-Star game. In the second inning he came to bat, something he hadn't done in years because of the American League's designated-hitter rule. He took a few uncertain practice swings and then looked out at his forbidding opponent, Dwight Gooden, who the previous year had won the Cy Young award.

Gooden wound up and threw a white-hot fastball past Clemens. With an embarrassed smile on his face, Clemens stepped out of the box and asked catcher Gary Carter, "Is that what my pitches look like?"

"You bet it is!" replied Carter.

From that day on, Clemens later said, with a fresh reminder of how overpowering a good fastball is, he pitched with far greater boldness.

Sometimes we forget the Holy Spirit within us and how powerful our witness can be.

–Craig Brian Larson

SOMETHING TO THINK ABOUT

Having thus chosen our course, let us renew our trust in God and go forward without fear and with manly hearts.

—

Abraham Lincoln

THE LIMITS OF AMBITION

AMBITION IS THE GREASE OF INDUSTRY. WITHOUT IT, NOTHING MOVES. YET SOME AMBITION CAN BE DESTRUCTIVE. THE APOSTLE PAUL HAD AN IVY-LEAGUE RESUMÉ, BUT HE COMMITTED HIMSELF TO SOMETHING GREATER THAN PERSONAL AMBITION. IN HIS LETTER TO THE PHILIPPIANS HE DESCRIBED HOW PASSION REPLACED AMBITION AS THE DRIVING FACTOR IN HIS LIFE.

PHILIPPIANS 3:7-11

But whatever was to my profit I now consider loss for the sake of Christ. What is more, I consider everything a loss compared to the surpassing greatness of knowing Christ Jesus my Lord, for whose sake I have lost all things. I consider them rubbish, that I may gain Christ and be found in him, not having a righteousness of my own that comes from the law, but that which is through faith in Christ—the righteousness that comes from God and is by faith. I want to know Christ and the power of his resurrection and the fellowship of sharing in his sufferings, becoming like him in his death, and so, somehow, to attain to the resurrection from the dead.

CHARACTER CHECK
Can I accomplish something without caring whether I get the credit?

_____

_____

_____

_____

_____

IN BUSINESS TERMS

It is ironic that I, who had little ambition, gained such influence, while others, who would kill to have this kind of effect, may still be seeking it. I don't think you find something by going directly at it.

When the Navy trained us to spot airplanes at night, they said the center part of your eye is blind at night. If you try to look directly at the sound at night, you never will see the plane. If you look to the right or the left of the sound, you'll see it out of the part of your eye that isn't night-blind. Ambition is like that.

People who pursue ambitious goals often are some of the most frustrated people in the world. And those who succeeded oftentimes have been ruthless in achieving it and have left bodies scattered over the landscape.

But for every one of the achievers–even the honest ones–there is an enormous number of people who years ago offered themselves for ministry and have never come close to achieving their goals. So we have to offer ourselves to God to do whatever he wants us to do, and let the ambition go by the way.

–Richard Nelson Bolles

SOMETHING TO THINK ABOUT

So many missionaries, intent on doing something, forget that God's main work is to make something of them.

—

Jim Elliot

PROGRESS, NOT PERFECTION

STRIVING FOR EXCELLENCE IN LIFE IS A WORTHY GOAL, BUT PERFECTION IS IMPOS-
SIBLE. EVEN THE APOSTLE PAUL RECOGNIZED THAT HE WOULD NEVER "ARRIVE" IN
THIS LIFE. BUT THAT DIDN'T DRIVE HIM TO DESPAIR. HE WAS WISE ENOUGH TO
REALIZE THAT WHILE IN THIS LIFE PERFECTION WOULD ELUDE HIS GRASP, HE COULD
FIND A PACE THAT WOULD AT LEAST ALLOW HIM TO REALIZE PROGRESS.

PHILIPPIANS 3:12-16

Not that I have already obtained all this, or have already been made perfect, but I press on to take hold of that for which Christ Jesus took hold of me.

Brothers, I do not consider myself yet to have taken hold of it. But one thing I do: Forgetting what is behind and straining towards what is ahead, I press on toward the goal to win the prize for which God has called me heavenward in Christ Jesus.

All of us who are mature should take such a view of things. And if on some point you think differently, that too God will make clear to you. Only let us live up to what we have already attained.

CHARACTER CHECK
Where is my drive to be perfect steering me wrong?

IN BUSINESS TERMS

Progress is more important than perfectionism.

Sometimes I invite leaders to do this exercise: "During the coming week, drive out near the middle of Nowhere. Pull your car over to the side of the road and have a last, pleasant conversation with that old, old friend, Compulsive Perfectionism. Then open the door of the car, shove gently, quickly close the door, and drive rapidly down the road.

"In about a mile, you will find three new friends–eager, smiling, hoping to be picked up. These three good friends are Progress, Pace, and Prayer. Fill your car–fill your life–with those three."

Effective leadership begins with the confidence that hope is stronger than memory, the open tomb stronger than the bloodied cross, the risen Lord stronger than the dead Jesus, Easter stronger than Good Friday, resurrection stronger than crucifixion.

–Kennon Callahan

SOMETHING TO THINK ABOUT

Anything worth doing is worth doing poorly.

—

G. K. Chesterton

ONE THING WORTH HAVING

GETTING FIRED AND EXPERIENCING JOY RARELY GO TOGETHER. ASKING SOMEONE TO "REJOICE ALWAYS" AFTER LOSING HIS JOB SEEMS CRUEL OR INSENSITIVE. BUT PHILIPPIANS 4 SHOWS THAT EVEN IN TRIALS, WE CAN EXPERIENCE JOY—NOT IN THE SENSE OF EARTHLY HAPPINESS, BUT IN THE UNEXPLAINABLE PEACE THAT GOD SENDS US.

PHILIPPIANS 4:4-7, 12b-13

Rejoice in the Lord always. I will say it again: Rejoice! Let your gentleness be evident to all. The Lord is near. Do not be anxious about anything, but in everything, by prayer and petition, with thanksgiving, present your requests to God. And the peace of God, which transcends all understanding, will guard your hearts and your minds in Christ Jesus....

I have learned the secret of being content in any and every situation, whether well fed or hungry, whether living in plenty or in want. I can do everything through him who gives me strength."

CHARACTER CHECK
In times of suffering, do I experience a strong sense of the presence of God?

_____

_____

_____

_____

_____

IN BUSINESS TERMS

Our oldest daughter died on May 13, 1995. The Bible tells us to rejoice always. How do you rejoice under those circumstances?

My wife and I are still weeping. However, we can rejoice in the total assurance we have that we know where she is and that we loved her and provided her the best medical care available. Psalm 139:16 says God set her death date from the foundation of the earth. In weeping we can still have joy, but joy is a condition we're in because of a decision we made.

In times of weeping, joy is the only thing in life worth having. Her death is the most difficult thing I've experienced, and yet I've felt God's presence so strong since then. It has brought me closer to the Lord than anything since my salvation.

–Zig Ziglar

SOMETHING TO THINK ABOUT

What soap is for the body, tears are for the soul.

—

Jewish proverb

THE GIFT OF SEX

SEX—IT ATTRACTS US AND FRIGHTENS US. ITS HIGHLY CHARGED FORCE HAS POTENTIAL FOR GREAT GOOD OR GREAT HARM. THE BIBLE IS CLEAR: SEX IS A GOOD GIFT DIRECT FROM GOD. BUT SEX GONE AWRY HAS THE POTENTIAL TO DESTROY US. OUTSIDE OF MARRIAGE, SEX DEVIATES FROM THE PURPOSES OF GOD, WHO CALLS US TO HOLINESS.

1 THESSALONIANS 4:1-8

Finally, brothers, we instructed you how to live in order to please God, as in fact you are living. Now we ask you and urge you in the Lord Jesus to do this more and more. For you know what instructions we gave you by the authority of the Lord Jesus.

It is God's will that you should be sanctified: that you should avoid sexual immorality; that each of you should learn to control his own body in a way that is holy and honorable, not in passionate lust like the heathen, who do not know God; and that in this matter no one should wrong his brother or take of advantage of him. The Lord will punish men for all such sins, as we have already told you and warned you. For God did not call us to be impure, but to live a holy life. Therefore, he who rejects this instruction does not reject man but God, who gives you his Holy Spirit.

CHARACTER CHECK
How can I begin cultivating proper attitudes about sex?

_____

_____

_____

_____

_____

IN BUSINESS TERMS

When I was involved in pornography, I experienced sex in its "disconnected" form, as a voyeur of other people's bodies, apart from relationship. My healing process will surely involve reconnecting that sexual power and energy with the growth toward intimacy it was designed to accompany.

British journalist G. K. Chesterton once likened this world to the desert island site of a shipwreck. A sailor awakes from a deep sleep and discovers treasure strewn about, relics from a civilization he can barely remember. One by one he picks up the relics–gold coins, a compass, fine clothing–and tries to discern their meaning. According to Chesterton, fallen humanity is in such a state. Good things on earth still bear traces of their original purpose, but each is also subject to misinterpretation or abuse because of fallen, "amnesiac" human nature.

Sexual desire, one of the world's most powerful "relics," invites obsession. When we experience sexual desires, it seems only right to follow where they lead. As the modern song puts it, "It can't be wrong when it feels so right."

The problem is that we are the problem. The good things on earth–food, drink, sex, recognition, power, wealth–are not spoiled; we are. They are relics of Eden. But our amnesia affects our ability to determine their proper use.

–Anonymous writer

SOMETHING TO THINK ABOUT

There is no getting away from it: the old Christian rule is "Either marriage, with complete faithfulness to your partner, or else total abstinence." Chastity is the most unpopular of the Christian virtues.

—

C. S. Lewis

THE TRYING-HARDER TRAP

EVERYONE HAS TO-DO LISTS, BUT FEW EVER CONSIDER A "TO-BE" LIST. GOD
REVERSES THE ORDER, PLACING BEING BEFORE DOING. BEFORE THE APOSTLE PAUL
EVER COUNSELED HIS YOUNGER COLLEAGUE, TIMOTHY, TO WORK HARD AT HIS MIN-
ISTRY, HE URGED HIM TO PAY ATTENTION TO HIS OWN PERSONAL LIFE—TO PUT
FIRST THINGS FIRST.

1 TIMOTHY 4:12-16

*Don't let anyone look down on you because you are young, but set
an example for the believers in speech, in life, in love, in faith and in
purity. Until I come, devote yourself to the public reading of Scripture,
to preaching and to teaching. Do not neglect your gift, which was given
you through a prophetic message when the body of elders laid their
hands on you.*

*Be diligent in these matters, give yourself wholly to them, so that
everyone may see your progress. Watch your life and doctrine closely.
Persevere in them, because if you do, you will save both yourself and
your hearers.*

CHARACTER CHECK
How well am I receiving God's grace?

_____

_____

_____

_____

_____

IN BUSINESS TERMS

My besetting sin is to think if I try just a little harder, I can get this right. Well, that's also Washington, D.C.'s problem: People here think they just need to try harder and they can make the thing work. Washington is a great town because you don't have to be a blueblood. You can come here from anywhere and make something of yourself as long as you're willing to work hard. But that is also why this is a dangerous town. It is easy to get confused about who the Savior is.

So it's no accident I keep talking about God's grace, which is all about God's initiative, not ours. You can't make grace happen. The lie our people hear all week long is "If you hustle, you can make it happen."

But the real question isn't, "How hard are you working?" but, "How well are you receiving?"

–M. Craig Barnes

SOMETHING TO THINK ABOUT

A man must completely despair of himself in order to become fit to obtain the grace of Christ.

—

Martin Luther

STAYING THE COURSE

No professional athlete can endure the hours of training, which is often boring and repetitive, and the injuries, which can nag him or her for months, without a deep sense of mission. The apostle Paul had an unwavering commitment to carry out his mission as a "herald and an apostle and a teacher." This enabled him, through great hardship, to stay the course.

2 TIMOTHY 1:6-9a, 11-12

For this reason I remind you to fan into flame the gift of God, which is in you through the laying on of my hands. For God did not give us a spirit of timidity, but a spirit of power, of love and of self-discipline.

So do not be ashamed to testify about our Lord, or ashamed of me his prisoner. But join with me in suffering for the gospel, by the power of God, who has saved us and called us to a holy life—not because of anything we have done but because of his own purpose and grace. . . . And of this gospel I was appointed a herald and an apostle and a teacher. That is why I am suffering as I am. Yet I am not ashamed, because I know whom I have believed, and am convinced that he is able to guard what I have entrusted to him for that day.

CHARACTER CHECK
Do I have a clear sense of what my mission is here on earth?

_____

_____

_____

_____

IN BUSINESS TERMS

I've been associated with a number of companies, and I've noticed that the most successful organizations, in terms of profits, impact on intended market, and team spirit among the employees, always had a clear sense of mission and purpose. In several cases the company mission statement hung in the reception area and on the wall of every department. They knew what they were–and weren't–about.

The less successful businesses seemed unclear on their purpose, beyond "sell more of product X." Staff was fuzzy about the senior management's vision; morale was low. They really didn't know what they were about.

The same holds true for individuals.

I've found it helpful to develop a statement of mission: What has God put me here for? What am I called and gifted to do? What can I uniquely offer?

So many good things compete for our time and attention that it's easy to scatter our efforts. A personal mission statement–or at least a thought-through, prayed-over, reality-tested sense of our unique purpose–helps us to focus our efforts, maximize our energies, and create in us a deeper understanding of who we are in Christ.

–Elizabeth Cody Newenhuyse

EYES ON THE ETERNAL

Professional athletes often credit their success to a coach in high school or college. But they don't mention the skills they learned from that coach as often as they mention the type of person the coach was. The coach functioned like a mentor, similar to the way the apostle Paul worked with Timothy.

2 TIMOTHY 3:10-15

You, however, know all about my teaching, my way of life, my purpose, faith, patience, love, endurance, persecutions, sufferings–what kinds of things happened to me in Antioch, Iconium and Lystra, the persecutions I endured. Yet the Lord rescued me from all of them. In fact, everyone who wants to live a godly life in Christ Jesus will be persecuted, while evil men and impostors will go from bad to worse, deceiving and being deceived. But as for you, continue in what you have learned and have become convinced of, because you know those from whom you learned it, and how from infancy you have known the holy Scriptures, which are able to make you wise for salvation through faith in Christ Jesus.

CHARACTER CHECK
Who in my sphere of influence would be a good candidate for me to mentor?

IN BUSINESS TERMS

Lifestyle mentoring defines the principles of living. Recently I heard a young man say, "My grandfather was everything to me. He loved me, and he taught me how to live." How fortunate to have an older person in one's life about whom you can say that.

As we look at the Scripture for lifestyle mentoring, we immediately think of Paul and Timothy. From the text I don't know how much skill Paul gave him as a missionary, but we do know Paul was an excellent sponsor. We know he was a father in the faith. He let Timothy observe him at work. Paul promoted him to the churches. In a broad sense, I would call Paul a lifestyle mentor to Timothy.

This type of mentoring is a kind of parenting, without the parental responsibilities. The responsibility is on the young person to observe correctly.

The responsibility of the lifestyle mentor is to be open, real, and personify consistently who he is so the young person receives a clear, consistent signal. The mentor must provide a comforting atmosphere in which the student feels free to ask any question he needs clarified.

A good mentor never ridicules a question. He may choose not to answer it, but he is careful never to ridicule, for questions are the pump that makes the answers flow.

–Fred Smith, Sr.

WINNING THROUGH WEAKNESS

"WEAKNESS, IF NOT DESPISED, IS NOT TOLERATED OR REWARDED. YET IN THE BIBLE, THE APOSTLE PAUL, PERHAPS THE GREATEST MISSIONARY OF THE CHURCH, SHOWS HIS HUMANNESS. AGING, JAILED, AND SICK, THE GREAT APOSTLE SOUNDS LONELY AND A BIT DISCOURAGED IN 2 TIMOTHY. HE FRANKLY TELLS HIS YOUNG FRIEND TIMOTHY THAT HE NEEDS HIM. PAUL IS VULNERABLE HERE—YET HIS VERY WEAKNESS GIVES HIS MESSAGE EVEN MORE POWER.

2 TIMOTHY 4:9-11, 16–18

Do your best to come to me quickly, for Demas, because he loved this world, has deserted me and has gone to Thessalonica. Crescens has gone to Galatia, and Titus to Dalmatia. Only Luke is with me. Get Mark and bring him with you, because he is helpful to me in my ministry. . . .

At my first defense, no one came to my support, but everyone deserted me. May it not be held against them. But the Lord stood at my side and gave me strength, so that through me the message might be fully proclaimed and all the Gentiles might hear it. And I was delivered from the lion's mouth. The Lord will rescue me from every evil attack and will bring me safely to his heavenly kingdom. To him be glory for ever and ever. Amen.

CHARACTER CHECK
How might this kind of openness draw me closer to God?

_____

_____

_____

_____

_____

IN BUSINESS TERMS

Unwittingly, perhaps unconsciously, we sometimes feel our titles, our positions, and our responsibilities mean we have to perform in the exact manner expected of us. In so doing we dehumanize ourselves.

Being vulnerable means we are standing totally open as a human being–not as a pastor, not as a senator, not as a leader, not as a follower–just as a human being. There is nothing that elicits response from people more than to feel they are dealing with someone who is on their level, who feels what they feel.

Richard Halverson once reminded me of this, saying, "I am more and more aware that Christ living in you is what really creates the ability to be sensitive and responsive to people."

I don't think the Lord taught anything to his followers that is not achievable. Christ did not say, "Come and follow me, but you'll never really make it because I'm God and you aren't."

–Mark O. Hatfield

FREEDOM TO DO GOOD

IN BUSINESS, THE ONLY THING THAT MATTERS IS RESULTS. BUSINESS PAYS FOR PER-
FORMANCE AND PENALIZES NONPERFORMANCE. BUT IN OUR SPIRITUAL LIFE, WE
CAN'T PERFORM TO EARN GOD'S GRACE. RATHER, GOD'S GRACE GIVES US THE FREE-
DOM TO RESPOND BY DOING GOOD.

TITUS 3:3-8

At one time we too were foolish, disobedient, deceived and enslaved by all kinds of passions and pleasures. We lived in malice and envy, being hated and hating one another. But when the kindness and love of God our Savior appeared, he saved us, not because of righteous things we had done, but because of his mercy. He saved us through the washing of rebirth and renewal by the Holy Spirit, whom he poured out on us generously through Jesus Christ our Savior, so that, having been justified by his grace, we might become heirs having the hope of eternal life. This is a trustworthy saying. And I want you to stress these things, so that those who have trusted in God may be careful to devote them-selves to doing what is good. These things are excellent and profitable for everyone.

CHARACTER CHECK
Do I understand the connection between grace and the freedom to fail?

_____

_____

_____

_____

_____

IN BUSINESS TERMS

Grace was genuine, real, personal, and palpable to the great saints. Brother Lawrence, Frank Laubach, François Fenelon–these Christian mystics had no doubt they were the constant recipients of God's amazing grace. Grace was a practical part of their everyday life. For example, Brother Lawrence said that when he made a mistake he didn't spend any time thinking about it; he just confessed it and moved on. He reminded God that without him, to fall is natural. Before I read that, I lingered over guilt. Immediate grace was too good to be true. Brother Lawrence's experience greatly released me.

Nevertheless, legalism appeals to our common sense. I find it necessary to remind myself that the very Scripture that makes me know my guilt lets me know God's grace. By refusing grace we play God and punish ourselves. We view events as punishment. We see discipline coming when in reality it isn't discipline, it's just a consequence, but we try to read into it God's judgment.

Why? Because we feel we deserve judgment rather than grace. Grace brings freedom. If we could only accept grace fully, then we could have the freedom to admit failure and move on. Since grace cannot be deserved, why should I feel others are more worthy of it than I?

–Fred Smith, Sr.

SOMETHING TO THINK ABOUT

Christ is no Moses, no exactor, no giver of laws, but a giver of grace, a Savior; he is infinite mercy and goodness, freely and bountifully given to us.

—

Martin Luther

SOLID RELATIONSHIPS

WHAT DOES ACCOUNTABILITY MEAN TO YOU? OTHERS POKING INTO YOUR PERSONAL BUSINESS? EFFECTIVE LEADERS UNDERSTAND THE VALUE OF ACCOUNTABILITY. IF BELIEVERS MUST SOMEDAY GIVE AN ACCOUNT TO GOD, THEN ENLISTING OTHER BELIEVERS FOR PRAYER SUPPORT AND ENCOURAGEMENT IN THE HERE AND NOW MAKES GOOD SENSE.

HEBREWS 4:12-13; JAMES 5:19–20

For the word of God is living and active. Sharper than any double-edged sword, it penetrates even to dividing soul and spirit, joints and marrow; it judges the thoughts and attitudes of the heart. Nothing in all creation is hidden from God's sight. Everything is uncovered and laid bare before the eyes of him to whom we must give account. . . .

My brothers, if one of you should wander from the truth and someone should bring him back, remember this: Whoever turns a sinner from the error of his way will save him from death and cover over a multitude of sins.

CHARACTER CHECK
Whom could I invite into an accountability relationship?

_____

_____

_____

_____

_____

IN BUSINESS TERMS

Christian leaders are often perceived as the ultimate model of spirituality. In the church, parishioners expect to see someone in the pulpit who has it all together. He or she is supposed to be the living example of Christ-likeness. In political and business life, one is not necessarily expected to be perfect, but he or she is often expected to know all the answers.

We have to accept those expectations and do our best to live with them, but we need to pray that we do not begin to believe what people say of us. I've found a good stabilizing measure is to form relationships of accountability. My wife and I belong to a group that includes four other couples in Washington. We get together once a month. It's a ministry of support but also a ministry of accountability.

–Mark O. Hatfield

SOMETHING TO THINK ABOUT

You never find yourself until you face the truth.

—

Pearl Bailey

_____

_____

_____

_____

_____

THE PURPOSE OF CHURCH

SUNDAY MORNING GOLF MAY SEEM MORE APPEALING THAN SUNDAY MORNING WORSHIP. THAT'S THE NATURE OF RECREATION. BUT THE BIBLE SHOWS WHY WE NEED TO WORSHIP. ONE REASON IS THE IMPORTANCE OF "MEETING TOGETHER"—BEING WITH AND ENCOURAGING OTHER FOLKS OF LIKE COMMITMENT AS A RESPONSE TO WHAT GOD HAS DONE FOR US IN JESUS CHRIST.

HEBREWS 10:19-25

Therefore, brothers, since we have confidence to enter the Most Holy Place by the blood of Jesus, by a new and living way opened for us through the curtain, that is, his body, and since we have a great priest over the house of God, let us draw near to God with a sincere heart in full assurance of faith, having our hearts sprinkled to cleanse us from a guilty conscience and having our bodies washed with pure water. Let us hold unswervingly to the hope we profess, for he who promised is faithful. And let us consider how we may spur one another on toward love and good deeds. Let us not give up meeting together, as some are in the habit of doing, but let us encourage one another–and all the more as you see the Day approaching.

CHARACTER CHECK
Who needs for me to step up to the plate?

_____

_____

_____

_____

_____

IN BUSINESS TERMS

When a friend of mine couldn't sell his home after a move, he decided to rent it out. Twice in three years, tenants broke the lease and skipped town after trashing the place, leaving my friend with thousands of dollars in repairs.

He tried to sell the house again, and it sat on the market for months while he made mortgage payments he couldn't afford. His credit cards maxed out, foreclosure became a possibility, and his stress was sky-high.

When he told his friends at church about his problem, within 48 hours:

His couples' Bible study gave him and his wife a check that more than covered their next mortgage payment, giving them more time to sell the house;

His Sunday school teacher–a realtor and financial adviser– prayed with him and his wife, encouraging them;

A church elder–an attorney my friend could never afford–spent 90 minutes on the phone, giving advice.

My friend was striking out, and the church stepped up to the plate. But it never could have happened if he hadn't put his pride aside and made his needs known.

–Mark Moring

_____

_____

_____

_____

_____

RISK TAKERS

THE GREATEST LEADERS IN ANY INDUSTRY ARE RISK TAKERS. THE FOLLOWING EXCERPT FROM THIS FAMOUS PASSAGE OF HEBREWS, OFTEN CALLED "THE ROLL CALL OF THE SAINTS," PRAISES MEN AND WOMEN WHO WERE WILLING TO TRUST GOD COMPLETELY, WHO SAID YES TO HIM EVEN THOUGH THEY KNEW THE RISKS INVOLVED.

HEBREWS 11:1-2, 7, 11-12, 31; 12:1

Now faith is being sure of what we hope for and certain of what we do not see. This is what the ancients were commended for. . . .

By faith Noah, when warned about things not yet seen, in holy fear built an ark to save his family. By his faith he condemned the world and became heir of the righteousness that comes by faith. . . .

By faith Abraham, even though he was past age–and Sarah herself was barren–was enabled to become a father because he considered him faithful who had made the promise. And so from this one man, and he as good as dead, came descendants as numerous as the stars in the sky and as countless as the sand on the seashore. . . .

By faith the prostitute Rahab, because she welcomed the spies, was not killed with those who were disobedient. . . .

Therefore, since we are surrounded by such a great cloud of witnesses, let us throw off everything that hinders and the sin that so easily entangles, and let us run with perseverance the race marked out for us.

CHARACTER CHECK
Where in my life am I still holding back from trusting God fully?

IN BUSINESS TERMS

I don't think God asks us true-or-false questions. I think he asks us yes-or-no questions when we try to get close to him. Lots of people say "True" to the Atonement, the Resurrection, the Second Coming, but that's like saying, "True, I believe in marriage." Not until you say yes to a person are you actually married.

So God's first question is not, "Do you believe in the concept of discipleship?" It is rather this: "Will you trust me with your life, yes or no?" That's what he said to Abram: "Will you leave the familiar, sell your house, pack up your goods, and move out?"

He didn't ask Mary whether she assented to the doctrine of the Incarnation; he said, "Will you be the unwed mother of the Messiah, even though you'll probably never be able to convince your parents, your neighbors, or the rabbi that you didn't have an affair? Will you trust me?"

As a church boy growing up, I said "True" a lot of times. But it wasn't until one night in 1945, while standing guard duty in a bombed-out building in Stuttgart, Germany, thinking very hard about my life and what I'd be going home to, that I finally said yes to God.

–Bruce Larson

SOMETHING TO THINK ABOUT

What is faith unless you believe what you do not see?

—

Augustine

GOD'S ROLODEX

NETWORKING IS A SURVIVAL SKILL IN BUSINESS. THOSE WHO DO IT WELL FIND JOBS AND ADVANCE QUICKLY. THE SKILL OF NETWORKING IS THE SKILL OF CONNECTING WITH THE MOVERS AND SHAKERS. THE BIBLE, HOWEVER, COMMANDS US TO NETWORK WITH THE BROKEN AND HELPLESS. THAT'S WHAT THE LORD REQUIRES OF US.

JAMES 2:5-10, 12-13

Listen, my dear brothers: Has not God chosen those who are poor in the eyes of the world to be rich in faith and to inherit the kingdom he promised those who love him? But you have insulted the poor. Is it not the rich who are exploiting you? Are they not the ones who are dragging you into court? Are they not the ones who are slandering the noble name of him to whom you belong?

If you really keep the royal law found in Scripture, "Love your neighbor as yourself," you are doing right. But if you show favoritism, you sin and are convicted by the law as lawbreakers. For whoever keeps the whole law and yet stumbles at just one point is guilty of breaking all of it. . . .

Speak and act as those who are going to be judged by the law that gives freedom, because judgment without mercy will be shown to anyone who has not been merciful. Mercy triumphs over judgment!

CHARACTER CHECK

Do I have regular contact with people who have less than I do?

_____

_____

_____

_____

_____

IN BUSINESS TERMS

Chicago Tribune columnist Bob Greene wrote a column explaining why he spends so much time reporting the stories of abused children. One day he was going back to his hotel after listening to court testimony of how a Wisconsin couple had locked their 7-year-old daughter in a dog cage night after night and how their 11-year-old son had walked barefoot and in tears to a police station in November to beg someone to help his sister.

When Greene returned to his hotel room and turned on the television, he saw a live press conference with Latrell Sprewell, the NBA player charged with allegedly choking his coach. Sprewell was holding a press conference to voice his objections to being thrown off his team.

Greene writes, "From what I could tell, there were more than a hundred reporters and broadcast technicians in the room. . . . If a well-known person like Sprewell can summon so many reporters to come listen to him just by announcing that he wishes to speak–that underlines the need for the most voiceless and powerless among us to have their stories reported. When they're children, they can't ask for anyone to listen; especially for a child locked in a dark basement in a dog cage, if we who report the news don't decide on our own to come pay witness, no one will ever know the difference."

To come pay witness to the downtrodden and broken is part of the job description of those who claim Christ as Lord.

–David L. Goetz

NO FEAR

PLANNING FOR RETIREMENT MAKES GOOD SENSE. YET MUCH OF THE ADVERTISING FOR MUTUAL FUNDS AND OTHER RETIREMENT SERVICES IS BASED ON FEAR—"SAVE NOW OR YOU WON'T HAVE ENOUGH LATER." EVEN IN A NATION OF ABUNDANCE, FEAR IS A UNIVERSAL HUMAN EMOTION. IN THE BOOK OF FIRST JOHN, HOWEVER, THE WRITER POINTS OUT THAT THE FREEDOM IN GOD'S LOVE DRIVES OUT FEAR.

1 JOHN 4:13-18

We know that we live in him and he in us, because he has given us of his Spirit. And we have seen and testify that the Father has sent his Son to be the Savior of the world. If anyone acknowledges that Jesus is the Son of God, God lives in him and he in God. And so we know and rely on the love God has for us.

God is love. Whoever lives in love lives in God, and God in him. In this way, love is made complete among us so that we will have confidence on the day of judgment, because in this world we are like him. There is no fear in love. But perfect love drives out fear, because fear has to do with punishment. The one who fears is not made perfect in love.

CHARACTER CHECK
How might the love of God allay my biggest fear?

_____

_____

_____

_____

_____

IN BUSINESS TERMS

I find two basal emotions. The positive one is love and the negative one is fear. Every other negative emotion is ancillary and can be traced to fear: I fear I'm not doing enough; I fear I've done the wrong thing; I fear I won't do the right thing. I fight the fear of inadequacy, of not getting the job done, of not being the kind of person I could be.

The answer is to get rid of my fear. But how do I do that? Well, I don't do it. God can do it through me. The key is we don't have enough faith in the Lord. Love is letting go of fear. And God is love. And perfect love casts out fear. If I don't love God enough to let go of my fears, then I try to handle them myself—and go on fearing.

In the Old Testament, Jacob was at the ford of the Jabbok. He had wronged his brother, and he felt such guilt and alienation he was afraid to meet him the next day. So he wrestled with God, wrestled with his fear. But then he embraced his fear—went right into the teeth of it—crossing the river and meeting his brother. I find myself embracing my own fear of mortality when I go into the hospital where someone is dying. I embrace my fear of producing less than my best on Sunday morning by going right up into that pulpit.

–Robert Hudnut

_____

_____

_____

_____

_____

CHOICE IS EVERYTHING

"IT'S NOT MY FAULT. I COULDN'T HELP IT"—THAT EXCUSE USUALLY DOESN'T PLAY
WELL AT WORK, BUT PEOPLE STILL USE IT. THE EXCUSE WON'T WORK IN
CHRISTIANITY, EITHER. THE BIBLE VIVIDLY TEACHES THAT WE CHOOSE TO LIVE
ACCORDING TO GOD'S WAYS OR CHOOSE TO TURN AWAY FROM HIM. AND OUR ETER-
NAL DESTINY HANGS IN THE BALANCE.

REVELATION 20:11-15

*Then I saw a great white throne and him who was seated on it.
Earth and sky fled from his presence, and there was no place for them.
And I saw the dead, great and small, standing before the throne, and
books were opened. Another book was opened, which is the book of life.
The dead were judged according to what they had done as recorded in
the books. The sea gave up the dead that were in it, and death and
Hades gave up the dead that were in them, and each person was judged
according to what he had done. Then death and Hades were thrown
into the lake of fire. The lake of fire is the second death. If anyone's name
was not found written in the book of life, he was thrown into the lake
of fire.*

CHARACTER CHECK
In what area of my life have I put up the shutters against God's grace?

_____

_____

_____

_____

_____

IN BUSINESS TERMS

People need to know that human beings are not built to last forever, that endless existence is a gift that only the born-again receive, and that those who don't qualify for heaven simply get snuffed out. It's a form of annihilationism.

My concept of hell is owed to C. S. Lewis, whose key thought is that what you have chosen to be in this world comes back at you as your eternal destiny; if you have chosen to have your back, rather than your face, to God–if you've chosen to put up the shutters against his grace rather than to receive it–that's how you will spend eternity. Hell is to live in a state apart from God, where all of the good things in this world no longer remain for you. All that remains is to be shut up in yourself.

In Jean-Paul Sartre's play *No Exit,* four people are in a room they can't leave, and they can't get away from one another. What Sartre presents is the ongoing, endless destruction of each person by the others. Though Sartre was an atheist, his nightmare vision of this process makes substantial sense to me as an image of hell.

–J. I. Packer

SOMETHING TO THINK ABOUT

The one principle of hell is, "I am my own!"

—

George MacDonald

SCRIPTURE REFERENCES USED

Old Testament

New Testament

SCRIPTURE REFERENCES USED

NOTES

NOTES

NOTES

NOTES

NOTES

NOTES

NOTES

NOTES